T0066282

Learn How to Play the Baritone

ASAP

Chord Solos for the
Baritone Ukulele

By Dick Sheridan

For Concert and Tenor Ukuleles too!

Cover Photo: Kala Model KA-ASAC-B

All Solid Acacia Baritone Ukulele

www.kalabrandmusic.com

ISBN 978-1-57424-317-8
SAN 683-8022

Typography and design by Charylu Roberts and O. Ruby Productions

Cover by James Creative Group

Copyright © 2015 CENTERSTREAM Publishing, LLC
P.O. Box 17878 - Anaheim Hills, CA 92817

www.centerstream-usa.com

Acknowledgments

Much appreciation is due to so many who figured in helping put this book together. Doug Collingwood came up with the idea. Jim Beloff offered initial motivation to go forward with it, and Sid Lipton provided the encouragement to see it through. Neil Novelli sharpened his finely honed editorial pencil. Sue Edmonds and Joe Steinman created the prototype chord frames. Jim Stacey supplied technical assistance, while Jeff Yaro generously produced a much needed computer upgrade. Charylu Roberts did more than her share with patience, ongoing support, and professional skill in layout and typography. Did I mention my parents? After all, it was they who put that first ukulele under the Christmas tree. And there are others—Ronny Schiff for her keen eye and suggestions—and students and fellow musicians alike, whose help and inspiration, direct and otherwise, is enormously appreciated. To all, a most sincere THANK YOU!

Dick Sheridan

About the Author

Dick Sheridan began playing the small soprano ukulele when he was a pre-teen. From there it was on to folk-style guitar, the larger baritone uke, then the tenor and 5-string banjos. His performance experience, numbering thousands of engagements, started with a college campus band and continues today with various groups and a Dixieland jazz band he has led and played banjo with for over 40 years. During much of this time, he has privately taught virtually all fretted string instruments, the ukulele always having been his favorite. Dick has taught hundreds of students, yet as a teacher he fully endorses the saying, "By your students you will be taught."

> *"A wan'dring minstrel I—*
> *a thing of shreds and patches,*
> *of ballads, songs, and snatches,*
> *and dreamy lullaby!"*
>
> —From Gilbert & Sullivan's operetta "The Mikado"

Table of Contents

Arrangements

How These Arrangements Came to Be

My fascination with the ukulele started indirectly when I was about five or six years old. My father had taken me to the 1939/40 World's Fair in Flushing Meadows, NY, and during the course of our visit we saw an exhibit called the Midget Village. There, everything was scaled down to Lilliputian size. The interior of one small house stands out in my memory, not so much for its tiny tables and chairs and diminutive contents, but for a guitar that was propped upright in a corner. Chances are that guitar was also reduced to baritone ukulele proportions.

I was transfixed by the hourglass shape of that instrument. For years afterwards I held on to its image and relentlessly coveted a guitar of my own. I'd paw through the pages of the Sears and Montgomery Ward catalogs looking at pictures of guitars—orchestral models, cut-away designs, folk styles—along with related supplies and equipment. I'd study the accompanying descriptions practically memorizing every word.

But no guitar was forthcoming. I'm sure I pestered my parents to buy one for me but to no avail.

Then, some years later while still a pre-teen, I received a small soprano ukulele and method book as a Christmas present. My parents didn't know the difference between a guitar and a uke, nor were they fully aware of how obsessed I was about a guitar. Still, a uke was better than nothing and I faced the challenge of making some music with it.

My parents both played the piano—we had an old Weber upright—so tuning the uke with their help and that of the instruction book was not a problem. All of the numbers in the book were from before the turn of the century, and the first tune I tackled was "Jingle Bells." It was a disappointment as were all of the other tunes. Above the melody, which was written in standard notation, there were diagrams consisting of vertical and horizontal lines representing the strings and frets of the instrument. Dots were placed on the lines to indicate where fingers were to be put. These dots and diagrams, of course, are what we fretted string instrument players know as "chord diagrams." But in this case, these were not chords but rather single notes (one dot per diagram) following the melody note for note for the entire tune. The task was laborious, an unrelenting succession of diagrams, and I soon lost interest.

Up on a closet shelf went the uke and the method book.

～

The following summer, most likely from boredom, I took the uke down from the shelf, managed to retune it, and started all over again to plod through the tunes. But soon I discovered that below the melody line there was a sparser array of diagrams, each displaying more than one dot—chord diagrams—CHORDS! And from that moment when I first strummed a chord and heard the multi-note harmony, I was hooked. The love affair was on, and now more than a half century later that love affair continues.

It wasn't long before I learned a few basic chord formations and figured out how to use these chords to accompany songs. Songbooks with uke chords were plentiful as were ukulele method books. Moreover, sheet music at that time often included chord symbols, sometimes with diagrams, although the tuning of the uke varied widely to allow those basic chords to adapt to different keys.

Eventually I did get a guitar. Efforts with it were concentrated on emulating Burl Ives, Pete Seeger, Richard Dyer-Bennet and other folk singers who preceded the folk revival of the 1960s. Throughout it all, however, the uke was ever present and a constant companion.

Radio and TV personality Arthur Godfrey was popular during this period. He was a good musician, often singing tunes and accompanying himself on the baritone uke. I always suspected that Remo Palmieri helped him with arrangements. Remo was the guitar player for the Archie Bleyer Orchestra, which was Godfrey's studio band.

Godfrey started a craze for baritone ukuleles. I received one (a Harmony brand) as a high school graduation gift. That instrument is with me yet and is the one on which all of the chord solos in this collection were arranged.

Along with a guitar, the baritone uke went with me to college, where because of its light weight and portability I frequently played it for football pep rallies, parties, and dormitory jam sessions. It was then that I discovered chord solos—that is, using chords to play both melody and harmony simultaneously. My first and only attempt was the song "Moonlight and Roses." I could get it started but couldn't complete it because I just didn't know enough chord inversions. That attempt to work up a chord solo lay dormant until many years later.

About this time in the mid-1950s, while I was in college, Dixieland jazz went through a revival. Campus bands sprang up all over and my college was no exception. Because I was known to play a uke, the assumption was that I could play a banjo, and I was recruited to join a campus contingent. I knew nothing about the banjo and initially strummed along on the baritone uke. More volume was needed, so a banjo mandolin was located, the pairs of double strings reduced to just single strings, and the instrument tuned like a ukulele.

This sufficed for a while until by chance I discovered a banjo in an antique store one Christmas vacation. I was looking for a beer mug to give to a classmate friend, but the moment I walked into the cluttered shop I spotted an instrument case under a table. When I opened the case and found it contained a banjo that apparently had never been played, I was euphoric. It was a vintage Lyric tenor banjo made by the Bacon & Day Company out of Groton, CT. The case was lined with red velvet, the outside covered with a brown leatherette material. The price was $35, which I didn't have. I dashed home, asked my father if he would buy the banjo for me as a Christmas present, he agreed, and that banjo, along with my high school graduation baritone uke, is with me still. So again, another Christmas with a present of a stringed instrument.

At first I tuned the banjo like the baritone uke, playing it with the campus jazz band. It wasn't long before I decided that if I was going to continue to play the banjo I should learn the correct tuning. So from baritone tuning DGBE, I converted to tenor tuning CGDA.

That was 50 years ago, and I've continued with the banjo and Dixieland ever since, leading an active local traditional jazz band for over 40 years.

But what about the baritone uke? Frankly, it languished for many years, playing second fiddle to the banjo. That is, until a private music student acquired a baritone uke on e-Bay and asked me if I could help him learn to play it. It didn't take me long to rekindle my affection for the instrument. Besides, with the tenor banjo I had renewed my interest in arranging chord solos, and it became apparent that the same could be done for the uke.

The chord solos in this collection are the result of that effort and a recaptured enthusiasm for an instrument that has brought me hundreds of hours of challenge, enjoyment and reward.

The arrangements that follow are an outgrowth of that musical journey which started at the World's Fair in 1940. The journey spans six decades of love for fretted instruments that has included not only the uke but also the guitar, the lute, 4- and 5-string banjos and mandolins.

I'm delighted to share some of these arrangements with you, and I wish you as much fun playing them as I have had putting them together. If you're a new player or unfamiliar with the baritone uke, be patient and don't be discouraged if some of the arrangements seem daunting at first. You'll soon find a repetition of chord shapes and sequences. By way of encouragement, let me say that working on chord solos has taught me more about music and the instrument on which they're played than I would ever have learned otherwise. Believe me, it's worth the effort.

They say that even if we have many loves in our life, one will stand out. In my case, musically speaking, it's the ukulele. I hope you, the reader, will share this affection and find a full measure of enjoyment in the following arrangements.

Now then, tune up, play on, have fun, and share the fascination!

An Explanation of Chord Diagrams

To the experienced player it is evident that the basic chord diagram represents the four strings and frets of the instrument. The vertical lines correspond to the strings which, reading from left to right, are string numbers 4–3–2–1 tuned to D–G–B–E for the baritone ukulele, G–C–E–A for the soprano, concert and tenor ukes. The horizontal lines are the frets. Dots are placed on the string lines to show where fingers are to be placed to make a chord.

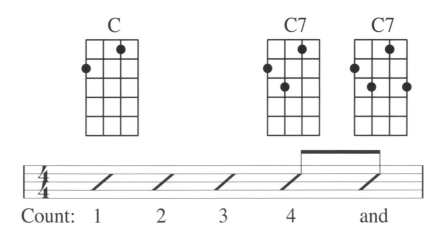

To the left and top of the diagram is a circle. When chord dots climb above the 5th fret a number is placed within the circle to represent the fret on which the top of the diagram is to be played. If no number appears in the circle the chord is played on the frets just as it appears on the diagram. Occasionally for clarification a fret number may be put in the circle even when the chord dots are below the 5th fret.

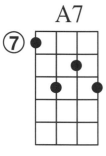

This chord is played on the 7th fret. Above the diagram is a symbol showing the name of the chord.

Below the chord diagrams are slash marks which show the number of strums that each chord is given. When a "beat" is divided in half, requiring two strums instead of one, the slash marks are connected. Often a new chord appears on the second strum of the divided beat.

The letters S/N that sometimes appear above the diagram mean "Single/Note." This is not a chord but an individual note whose location on the fretboard is shown below the diagram represented by two numbers separated with a diagonal such as 1/5. The first number is the string number, the second the fret to be played on that string. Often an S/N is contained within the preceding or following chord shape and can be played without lifting the fingers.

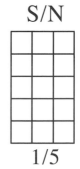

This single note would be played on the 1st string, 5th fret.

Another symbol looking like a tilted mathematic division sign consists of a diagonal line above and below which are dots. In conventional music usage this would indicate that a measure is to be repeated, but for our purposes it means simply to repeat the previous chord shape for the number of strums indicated.

Chord repeat sign:

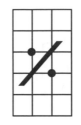

Sometimes the same chord shape is held (repeated) but moved to a different fret. Both chords have the same shape:

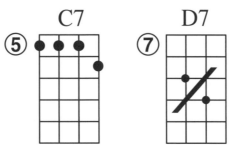

When a heavy line is run across the strings at a certain fret it means the index finger barres across all the strings at that position. This is a form of shorthand that shows a barre that might not otherwise be apparent from the dots. A partial barre is sometimes indicated connecting two or more dots.

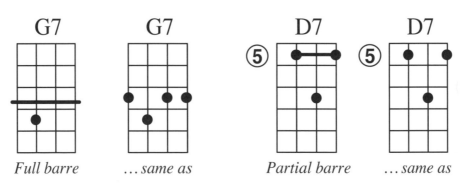

Barres are also implied with chord shapes having three or four dots on the same fret:

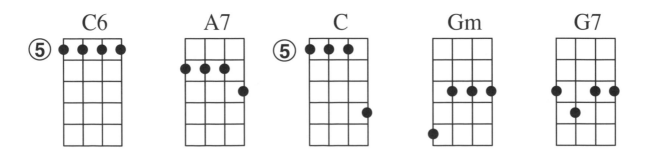

Something I call a "phantom dot" is an open circle dot instead of a solid one. This indicates that the dot is to be fingered but its sound is overridden by another dot (a solid one) higher up on the same string.

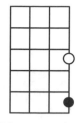

Phantom dot

A letter X placed on a string indicates that the string should not be played.

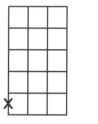

*Don't play on
4th string*

*Don't play on
1st string*

Some General Comments

Most of the chords used in the solos of this collection carry the melody on the 1st string. If the melody stretches beyond a reasonable range of the fingerboard, "octave jumps" are employed which preserve the melody but place it an octave above or below its normal position.

Whenever possible the melody is played as originally written. Occasionally, however, slight modifications are introduced to make playing easier. Time values may be increased so that eighth notes become quarters, halves to wholes, etc. But in all cases the essential sense of melody, harmony and rhythm is preserved.

Ukulele Tunings

There are four sizes of ukuleles. Ranging from the smallest to the largest they are soprano, concert, tenor and baritone. The three smaller sizes are usually tuned to so-called standard or C tuning: GCEA, with the G tuned higher than C in the familiar "My Dog Has Fleas" sequence. (An alternate tuning called D tuning raises the pitch a full tone for each string: ADF♯B.) The baritone is tuned like the top four strings of the guitar: DGBE, with the D pitched below the G string.

All of the chords in this collection of solos are named using baritone ukulele tuning. The chords and solos, however, can also be played on the tenor uke, and many on the concert. The chord shapes and their position on the fingerboard would remain the same, and although the *type* of chord would remain the same—major, minor, seventh, etc.— the letter name of the chord would be different. The chart below shows how the letter names would change:

Baritone Tuning	Concert and Tenor in C	Concert and Tenor in D
DGBE	GCEA	ADF♯B
A	D	E
B	E	F♯
C	F	G
D	G	A
E	A	B
F	B♭	C
G	C	D

Thus, an Am7 chord for the baritone would be a Dm7 chord in C tuning and an Em7 in D tuning. Similarly, a D7 Chord for the baritone would be a G7 for C tuning and an A7 for D tuning.

Some Terms, Symbols, and Abbreviations

Capo • (literally "head"), the beginning of a piece.

Coda • (literally "tail"), a concluding passage. This is the Coda symbol: ⊕.

Fine • (literally "end"), the conclusion.

D.C. • *da capo* ("from the head"), from the beginning.

D.S. • *dal segno* ("from the sign"). The sign is often 𝄋.

D.C. al Coda • *da capo al coda*. Go from the beginning to the Coda (⊕).

D.C. al Fine • *da capo al fine*. Go from the beginning to the Fine.

D.C. al Segno • *da capo al segno*. Go from the beginning to the 𝄋 sign. From the sign there may be a direction to proceed to a Coda (⊕).

D.S. al Coda • *dal segno al coda*. Go from the 𝄋 sign to the Coda (⊕).

D.S. al Fine • *dal segno al fine*. Go from the 𝄋 sign to the Fine.

X • don't play the string marked with an X.

Repeat signs • Double vertical bars with double dots enclosing a passage to be played again (𝄆   𝄇). If the repeat is back to the beginning no repeat sign is placed at the beginning.

Endings • When a section is repeated it may have different endings. The *1st ending* is enclosed within a bracket (⌐1.   ⌐) followed by a repeat sign (𝄇). The *2nd ending* (⌐2.   ⌐) replaces the first and is marked with either an open-end bracket or a closed one. There can also be a *3rd ending* which often is the same as the second ending (⌐2., 3.   ⌐).

The Songs

AURA LEE

(1861)

Words by W.W. FOSDICK
Music by GEORGE R. POULTON

One of the most popular ballads of the American Civil War, "Aura Lee" has undergone a good many adaptations and parodies over the years. Most noteworthy is Elvis Presley's "Love Me Tender." The lyrics are credited to Presley and Vera Matson, but Presley never really wrote the words to any of his songs. The lyrics were actually penned by Matson's husband, Ken Darby. Presley's recorded version was released as a single in 1956 and was featured later that year in a film of the same name. The song sold a million copies and hit the #1 spot on the *Billboard* charts following Presley's hit single, "Hound Dog."

Yet another adaptation is "Army Blue," which is associated with the U.S. Military Academy at West Point.

Humorist Allan Sherman, who created and hosted the TV game show *I've Got a Secret*, gave the melody his daft treatment with this unforgettable parody:

Every time you take vaccine,

Take it Aura Lee. (orally)

As you know the other way

Is more painfully.

Aura Lee

Baritone Ukulele

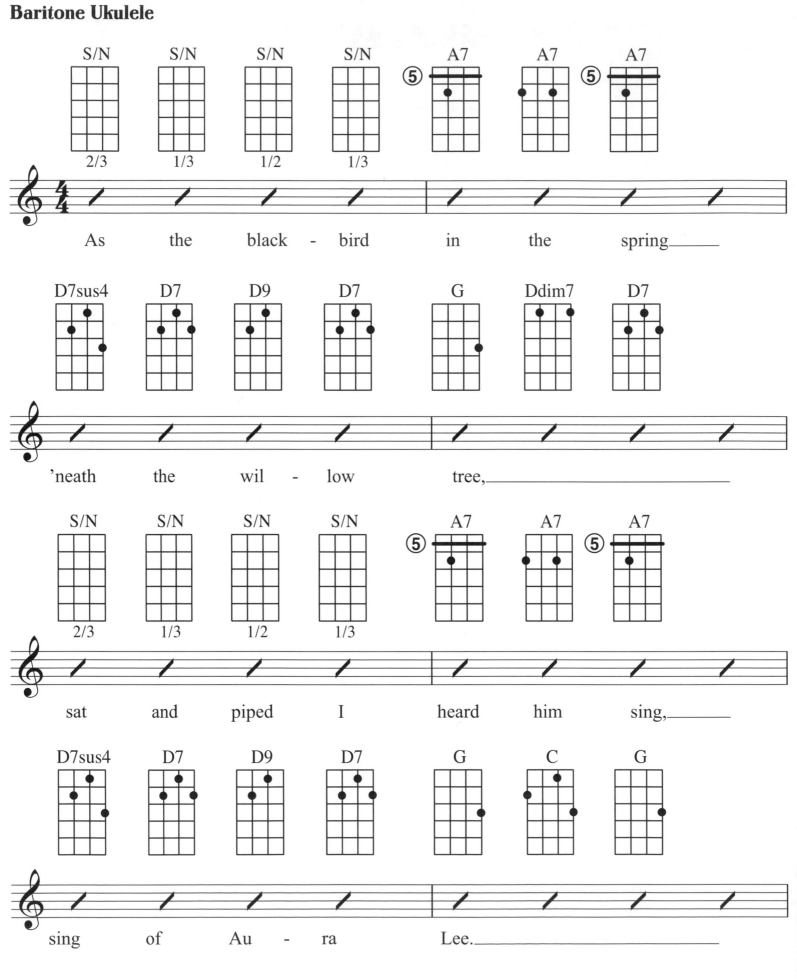

As the black - bird in the spring_____

'neath the wil - low tree,_____

sat and piped I heard him sing,_____

sing of Au - ra Lee._____

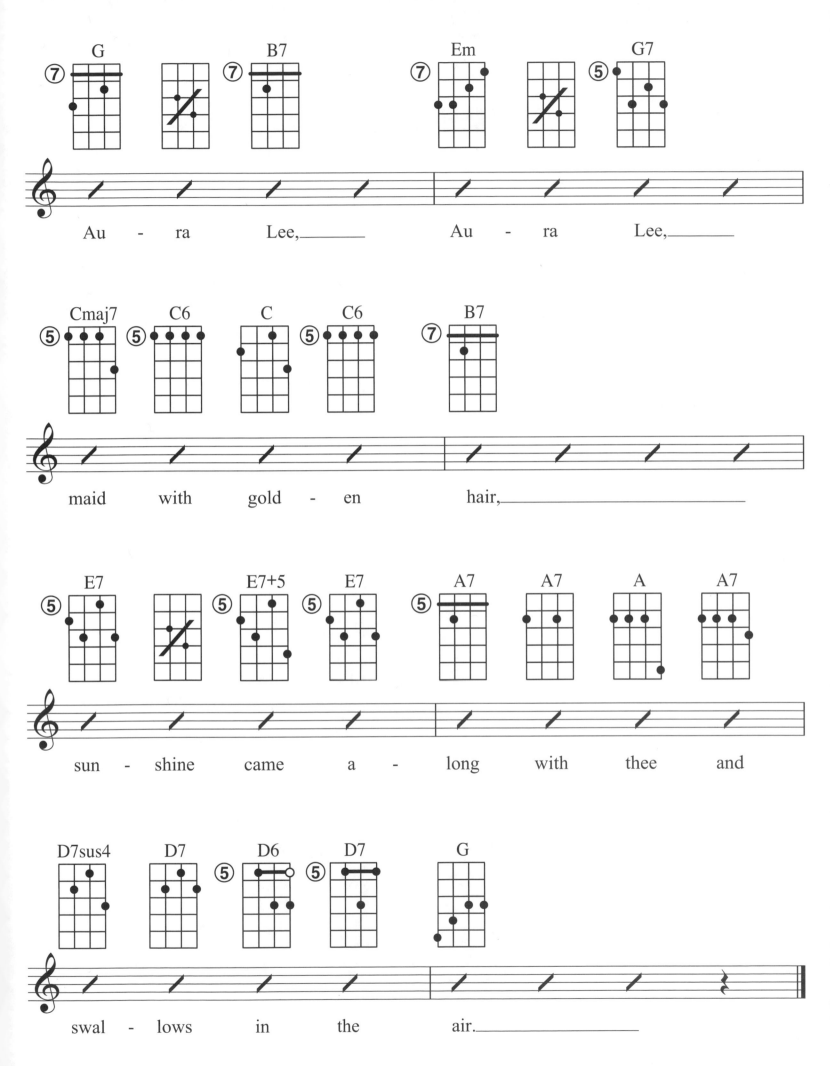

CARELESS LOVE

Traditional

It is not unusual for folk songs to cross over to the field of popular music. They are played by symphonies, performed as "art songs," arranged for big bands, crooned by lounge lizards in glitzy nightclub settings, even "jazzed up" in the repertories of swinging combos. But when is a folk song no longer a folk song? Is identity lost with these crossovers? Perhaps, but maybe not if the basic melody, harmony, words and rhythm remain substantially unchanged. By their very nature folk songs are seldom static. The framework endures but variants occur. Would you agree that a shift from the traditional to the mainstream is just another step in the evolutionary process?

Arthur Godfrey

Careless Love

Baritone Ukulele

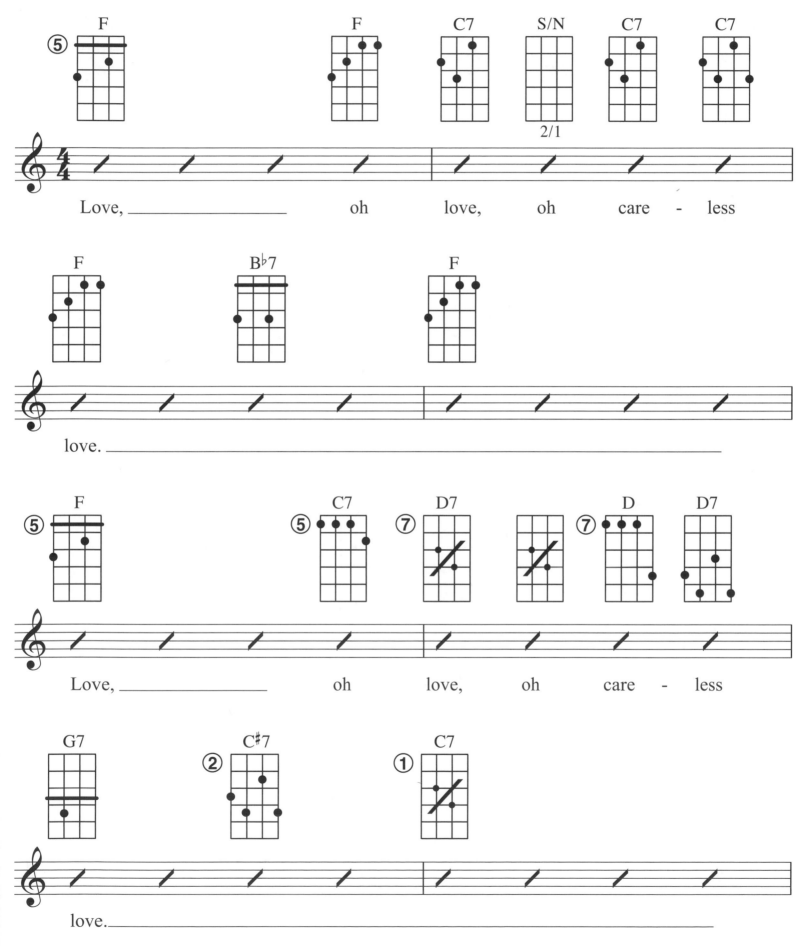

Love, _____ oh love, oh care - less

love. _____

Love, _____ oh love, oh care - less

love. _____

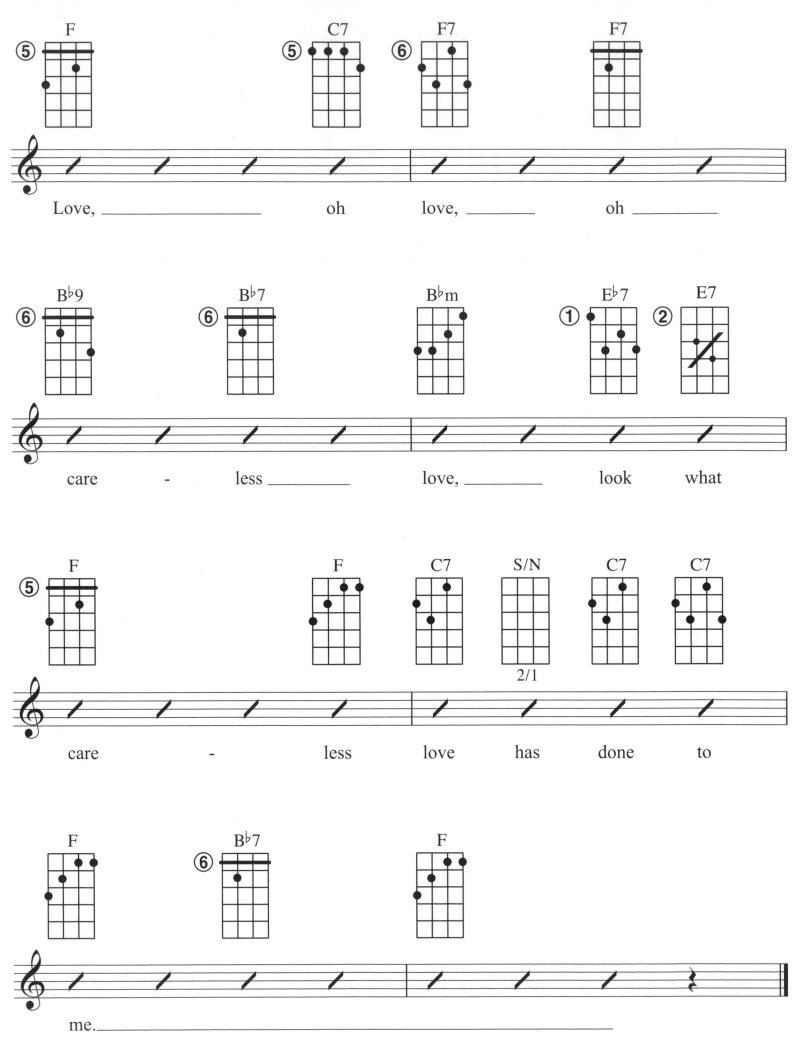

DARK EYES

(1884)

Music by FLORIAN HERMANN

What comes to mind with this haunting minor melody? A Russian Gypsy playing a 3-string balalaika? The Red Army Chorus, their bass-rich voices thundering out the opening lyrics "Occhi chornye, occhi stratstnye?"

What could be more Russian! Yet surprisingly, the song is not Russian at all. The lyrics were written by a Ukrainian poet in 1843, the words set to music and published twenty years later by a German composer.

We know the song by its present title, although the original words might be more correctly translated as "Black Eyes." Understandably this is perhaps too suggestive of some form of fisticuffs, perhaps a boxing match, a street brawl, or a marital slugfest instead of a romantic ballad. Jazz guitarist Django Reinhardt, himself a Gypsy living in France, recorded the song several times under the French title of "Les Yeux Noirs." With the song's universal popularity, surely there are many other translations in a variety of world languages.

Since the original lyrics and transliterated Russian words would be impossible for most of us—and the English lyrics in various translations are not much better—they are abandoned here and only the music is included.

Django Reinhardt jams with Harry Volpe

Dark Eyes

Baritone Ukulele

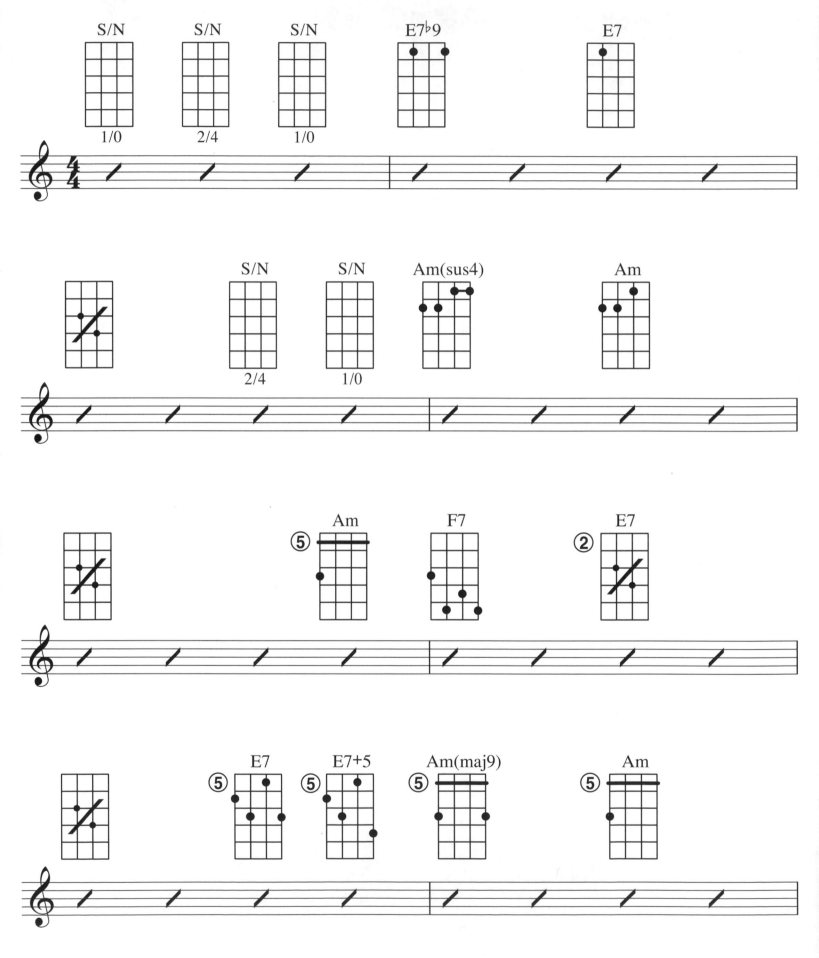

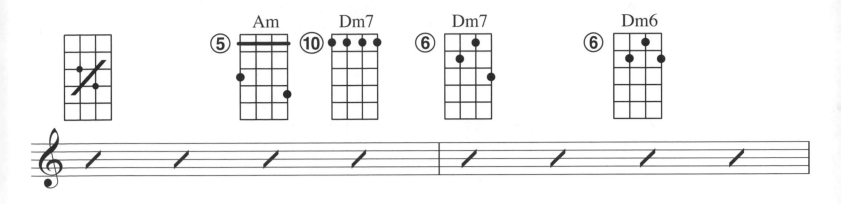

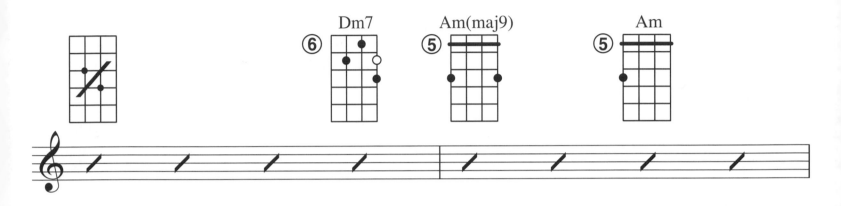

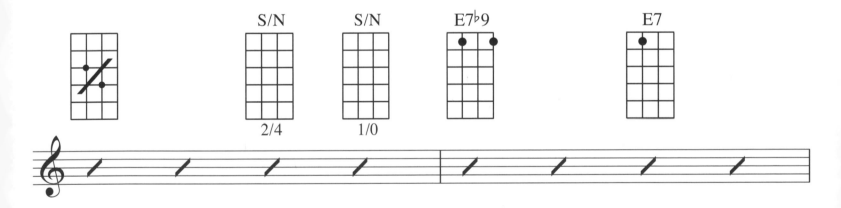

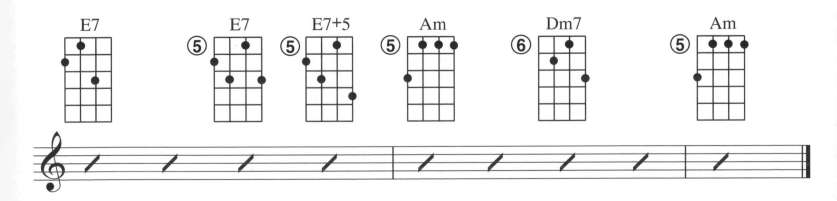

DEAR OLD GIRL

(1904)

Words by RICHARD HENRY BUCK
Music by THEODORE MORSE

Songs have always marked the rites of life's passage, the good and the bad, the happy, the sad. Following the Civil War and through the turn of the century, songs of sentimental sadness gained particular popularity. One common theme was the loss of youth ("Silver Threads Among the Gold," "When You and I Were Young, Maggie," "When You Were Sweet Sixteen.") There were the nostalgic longings for days gone by ("Down by the Old Mill Stream," "Back Home Again in Indiana.") Yet nothing touched the heartstrings so much as songs that sentimentalized the passing of life. There are many, including "Grandfather's Clock," "Asleep in the Deep," and "Danny Boy." But among the many, "Dear Old Girl" comes to the forefront. The heart-wrenching lyrics are softened by a lovely melody that moves poignantly between major and minor. Truly a bittersweet song that so easily can bring a tear to the eye.

Dear Old Girl

Baritone Ukulele

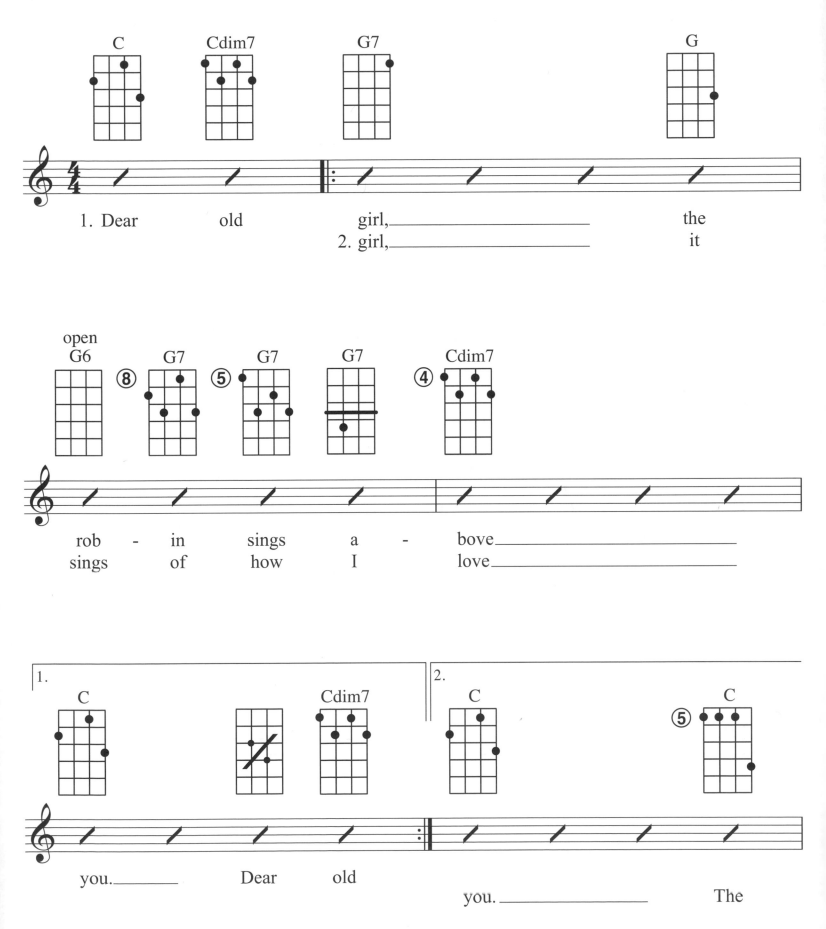

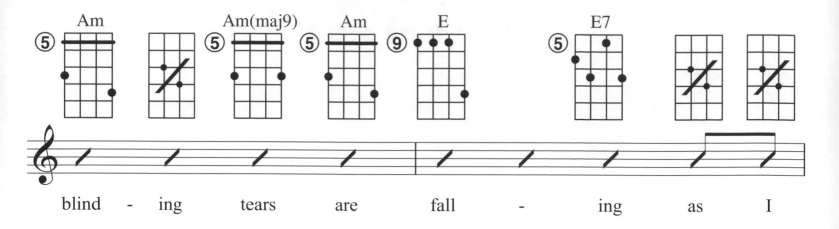

blind - ing tears are fall - ing as I

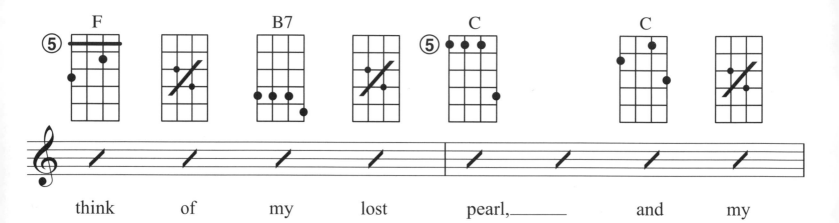

think of my lost pearl,_____ and my

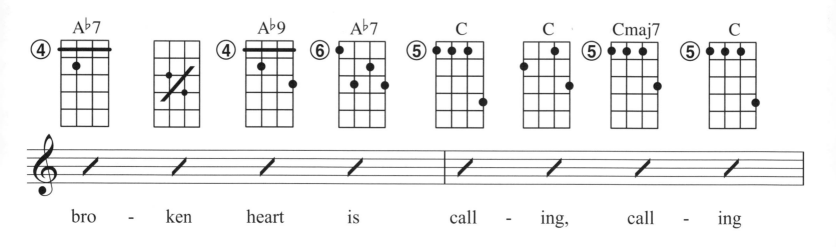

bro - ken heart is call - ing, call - ing

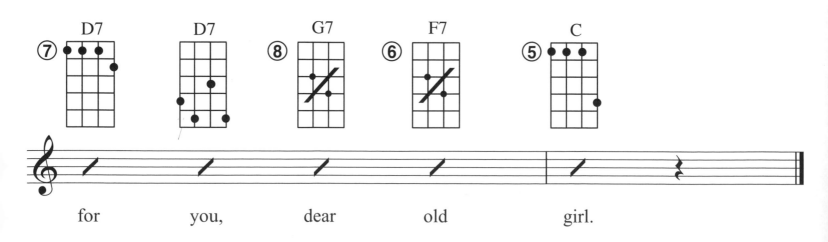

for you, dear old girl.

DOWN BY THE OLD MILL STREAM

(1920)

Words and Music by TELL TAYLOR

One of the most successful outpourings of Tin Pan Alley, this song has been printed and recorded many millions of times and is unquestionably among the best known of all barbershop quartet numbers. Its author, Tell Taylor, was a farm boy from Findlay, Ohio who swam in the Blanchard River near the site of the old Misamore Mill that was to become the inspiration for the song.

From a background of rural school teaching and singing with church choirs and for local social occasions, Tell moved on to performance in musical comedies and a career in vaudeville. He formed his own publishing company in Chicago and is credited with writing more than 20 songs, although none ever achieved the success of "Down by the Old Mill Stream." He died in 1937 en route to the West Coast where he was to assist in the production of a movie based on the song.

Playing Note: The timing may seem a little confusing in the measures with the Dm chord and following C#7. Strum each chord with five beats followed by three eighth notes. If the time were 6/8, count each chord as 1-2-3-4-5-&-6-& with beats 1 and 4 accented.

Arthur Godfrey and the Chordettes

Down by the Old Mill Stream

Baritone Ukulele

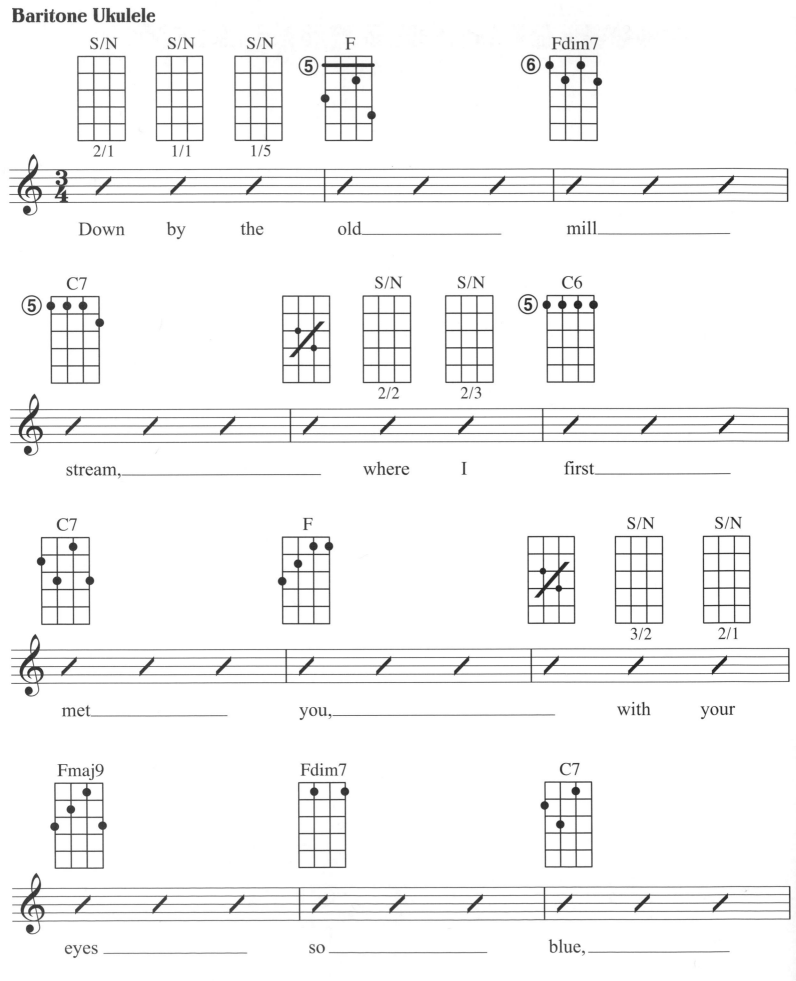

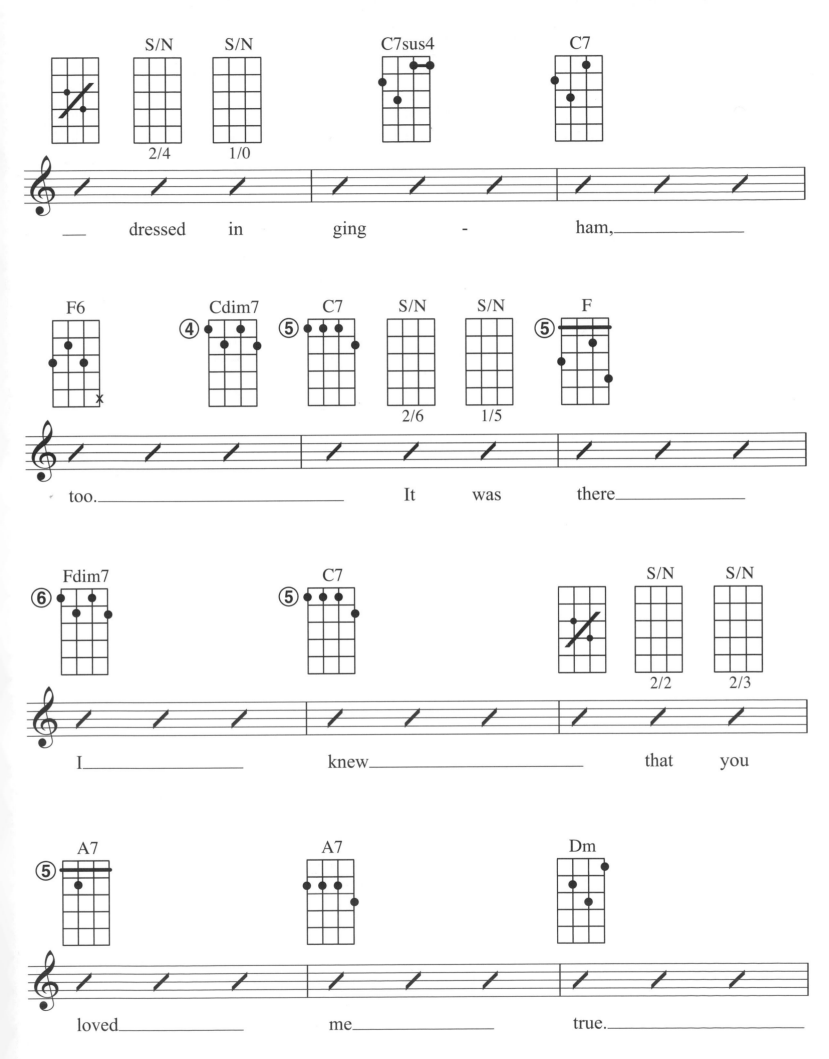

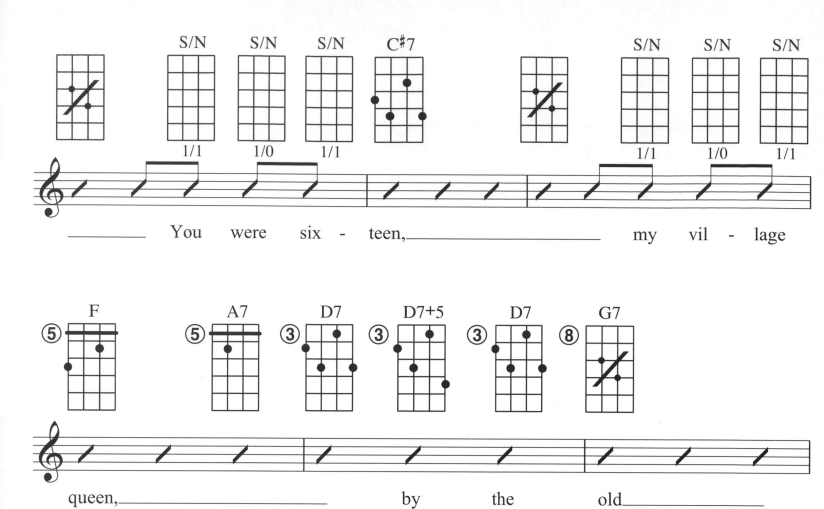

_____ You were six - teen, _____ my vil - lage

queen, _____ by the old _____

mill _____ stream. _____

Tag

(The old mill stream.)

GO DOWN, MOSES

Traditional

Although the Israelites had once been welcomed in ancient Egypt, as their numbers increased the pharaohs feared their strength and the possibility that they might align with an enemy in time of war. As a consequence, the Egyptians held the Hebrews in cruel captivity for some four hundred years, subjecting them to brutal slavery and oppressive forced labor.

According to the bible's *Book of Exodus*, Moses was charged with confronting the reigning pharaoh to plead for the release of his people from bondage, and to allow them to leave Egypt. Pharaoh was obstinate. The entreaties of Moses went unheeded.

It was only after ten terrible plagues were imposed on the Egyptians—the last being the slaughter of every one of their firstborn male children—that Pharaoh relented.

The homes of the Israelite slaves were spared from the slaughter, and that event—the Passover—has been celebrated by Jewish families ever since.

Many spirituals and hymns have had significance for African Americans in their struggle for equality and freedom. From the time of the Civil War, "Go Down, Moses" was just such a spiritual, and its words have resonance even today for all people who suffer the oppression of persecution and enslavement.

Go Down, Moses

Baritone Ukulele

When   Is - ra - el   was   in

E - gypt   land, _____   let   my   peo - ple

go. _____   Op - pressed   so   hard   they

could   not   stand, _____   let   my   peo - ple

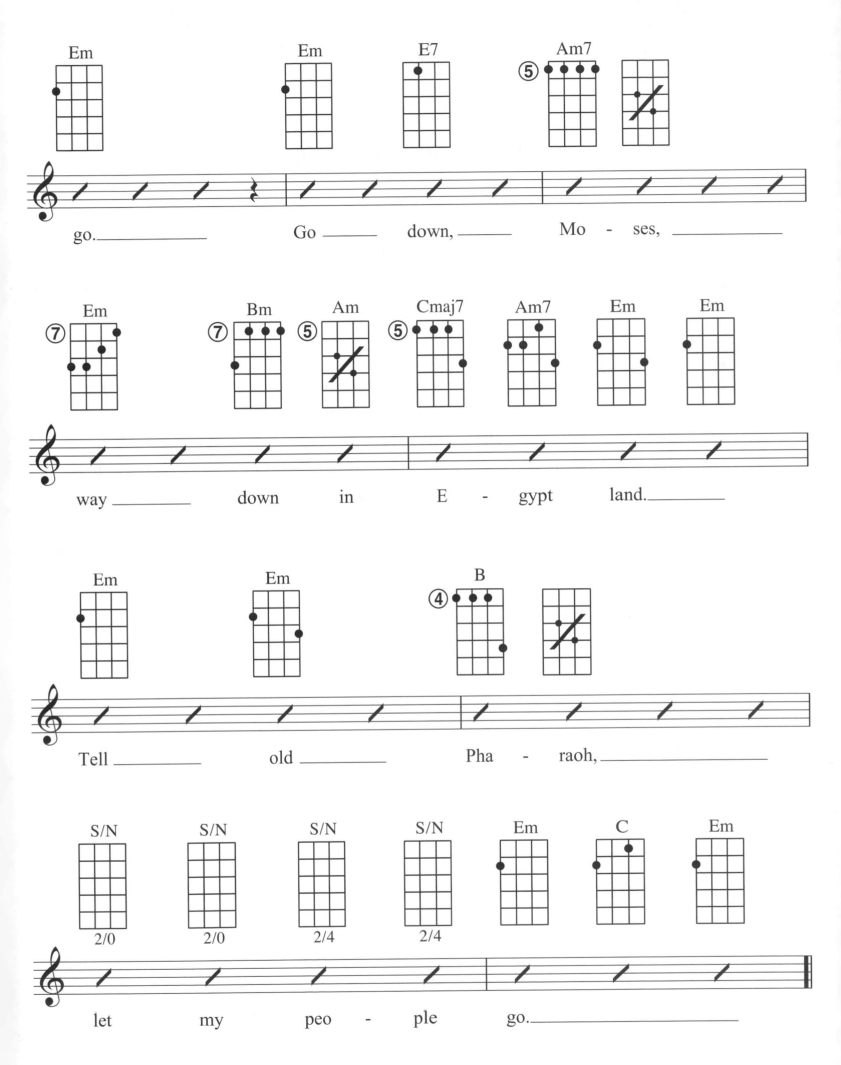

GRACEFUL AND EASY

(1899)

Words by DAVE REED
Music by FERDINAND SINGHI

It took a lot of digging to rediscover this song vaguely remembered from my youth. (Having forgotten the exact title didn't help.) Eventually in rummaging through dust-covered family heirlooms, I found it contained in a little 6x9 inch songbook folio from the 1930s. The internet could locate only one listing, a recording by a Bowdoin College vocal group. Further search with the help of the music libraries of Yale and Brown universities revealed the song's African American roots as a "cakewalk" song entitled "No Cake Comes Too High for Me." Apparently a barbershop and collegiate glee club favorite, as with many songs only its chorus has survived. The words out of context don't make much sense, but the music certainly does. As much fun to play on the ukulele as it is to harmonize with the boys… or the gals.

The Cake-Walk or Cakewalk was a dance developed from the "Prize Walks" held in the late 19th century, generally at get-togethers on slave plantations in the Southern United States. Alternative names for the original form of the dance were "chalkline-walk", and the "walk-around". At the conclusion of a performance of the original form of the dance in an exhibit at the 1876 Centennial Exposition in Philadelphia, an enormous cake was awarded to the winning couple. Thereafter it was performed in minstrel shows, exclusively by men until the 1890s. The inclusion of women in the cast "made possible all sorts of improvisations in the Walk, and the original was soon changed into a grotesque dance" which became very popular across the country

Graceful and Easy

Baritone Ukulele

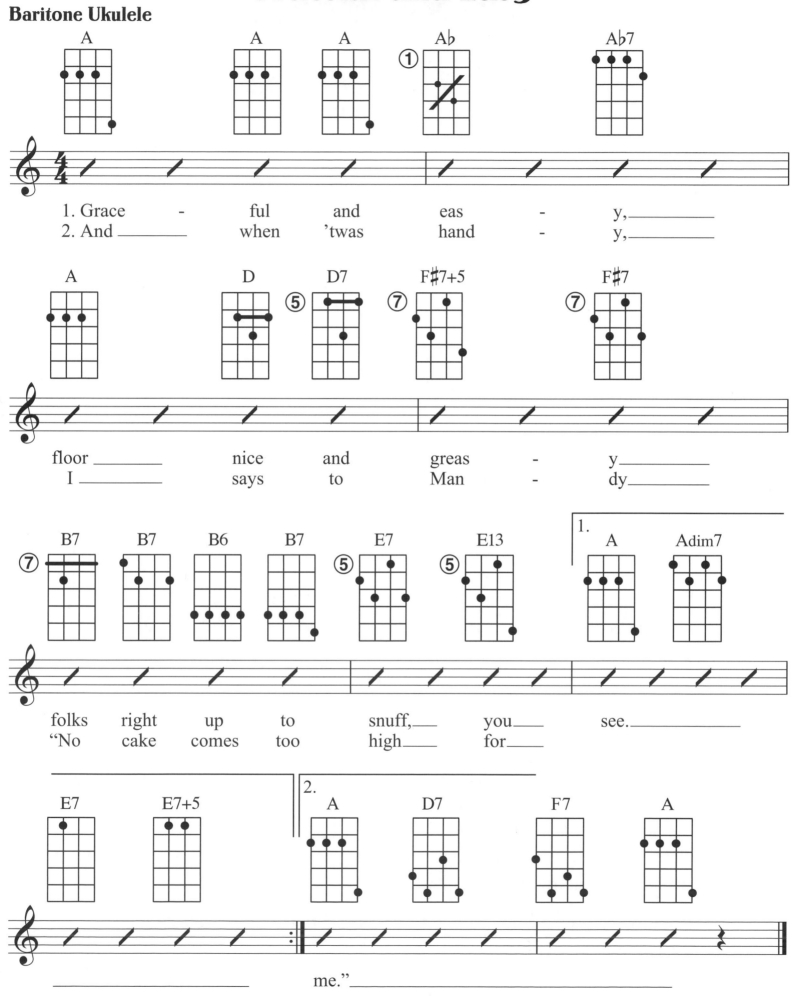

1. Grace - ful and eas - y,_____
2. And _____ when 'twas hand - y,_____

floor _____ nice and greas - y_____
I _____ says to Man - dy_____

folks right up to snuff,___ you___ see._____
"No cake up comes too high___ for___

_____ me."_____

GYPSY LOVE SONG

(1898)

Words by HARRY B. SMITH
Music by VICTOR HERBERT

When the nineteenth century rolled into the twentieth, Victor Herbert was truly ranked as the most prolific and celebrated contributor to the Broadway musical theater. In addition to his many songs, several operas, stage scores, and numerous instrumental arrangements for bands, orchestras, and choral groups, he is also credited with having written the first original screen score with the background music for the 1916 film, *The Fall of a Nation."* Of his 43 operettas, one of the most successful was *The Fortune Teller*, in which appeared the lovely, sentimental "Gypsy Love Song."

Victor Herbert was born in Dublin, Ireland, but when his father died, Victor and his mother moved to the home of her father in England. It was a stimulating, creative environment whose artistic influence stayed with him throughout his life.

Following formal studies in Europe and several years of active performance in Germany and Austria, Victor relocated to New York where he was engaged as a cellist with the Metropolitan Opera. It wasn't long before his emerging talent led him in other directions, and he began actively composing, conducting and appearing as a soloist.

With the great popularity at the time of operettas and light comedy operas, Victor's interest shifted from serious symphonic works to those for the musical theater. By nature he was light hearted and jovial, and he had a keen ear for lilting melodies and rich harmonies. These traits stood him in good stead as he devoted the sum of his efforts to the Broadway stage where he rapidly gained recognition and success.

As with many of his colleagues, Victor was concerned about the performance of copyrighted works without payment of royalties to composers. A suit against a New York restaurant resulted in a favorable Supreme Court decision. The protection against copyright infringement continues to this day through such organizations as ASCAP (American Society of Composers, Authors, and Publishers) of which Victor Herbert was a founding member in 1914.

Another favorite song by Victor Herbert, "Toyland," is also included in this collection of chord solos.

Gypsy Love Song

Baritone Ukulele

1. Slum - ber _____ on, _____ my
2. Can _____ you _____ hear _____ me,

lit - tle gyp - sy sweet - heart, _____
hear me in that sweet dream - land, _____

dream _____ of the field _____ and the

grove._____ where _____ your _____

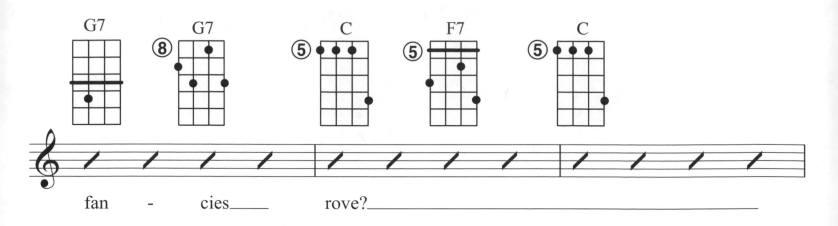

fan - cies____ rove?_____

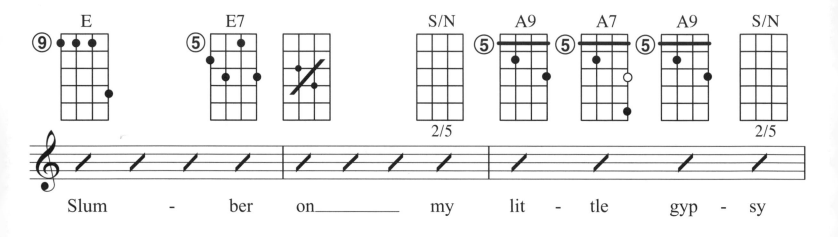

Slum - ber on_____ my lit - tle gyp - sy

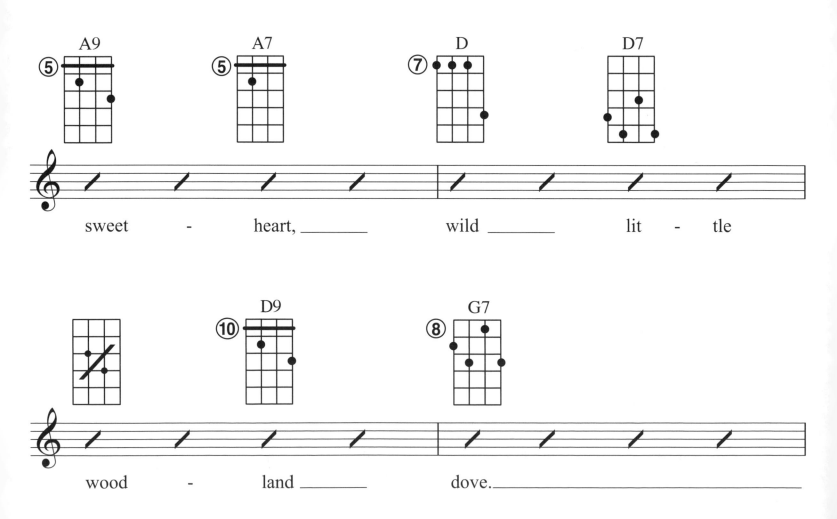

sweet - heart, _____ wild _____ lit - tle

wood - land _____ dove._____

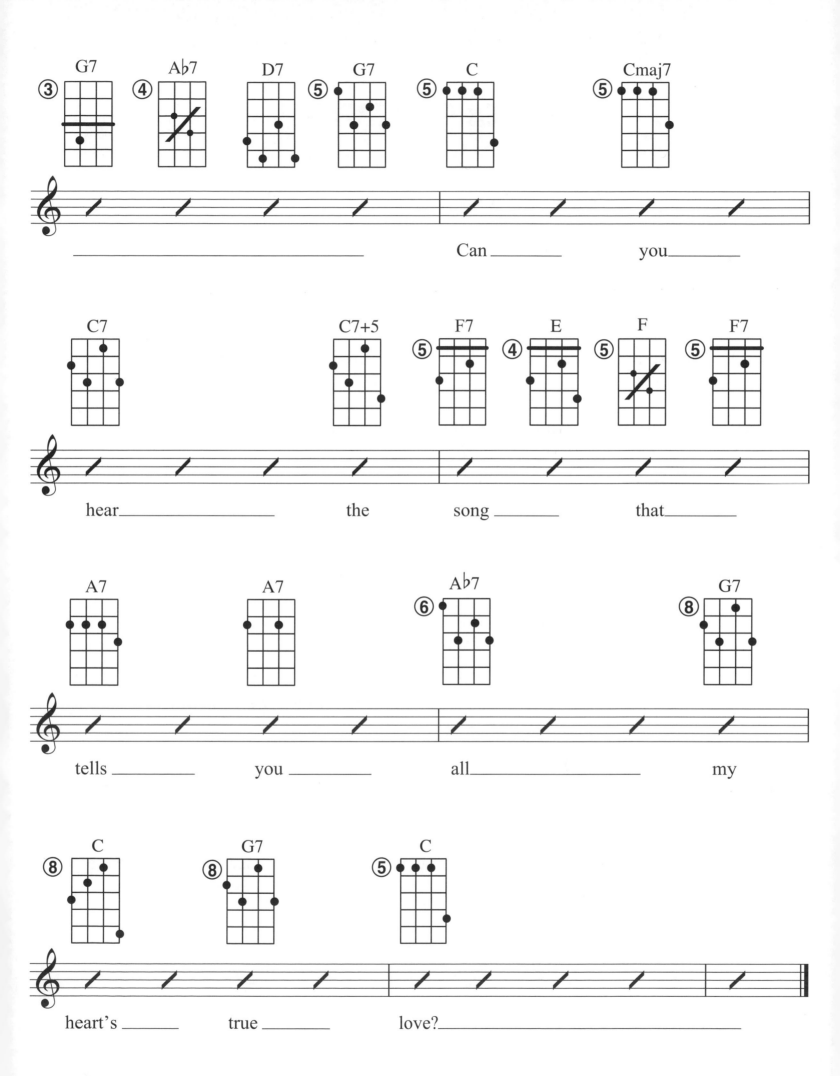

Can _____ you_____

hear_____ the song _____ that_____

tells _____ you _____ all_____ my

heart's _____ true _____ love?_____

HARD TIMES

(1854)

Words and Music by STEPHEN C. FOSTER

No songwriter is dearer to American hearts than Stephen Foster. His output of over 200 works includes a vast array of enduring favorites—sentimental love songs, poignant parlor ballads, and lively numbers from the blackface minstrel stages. How depleted our treasury of popular music would be without his "Oh! Susanna," "Camptown Races," "Beautiful Dreamer," and "Jeanie with the Light Brown Hair."

Many of Foster's songs were linked with the South even though he had visited there only once briefly. He was especially sensitive to the plight of plantation slaves, and his songs often reflected their dialects, but always with respect and affection.

Surprisingly for a song written over 150 years ago, "Hard Times" still has relevancy today. Contemporary performers like Emmylou Harris, Bob Dylan, Johnny Cash, and Bruce Springsteen have picked up on its haunting melody and troubling message. Consider the second verse:

> *While we seek mirth and beauty and music light and gay,*
> *There are frail forms fainting at the door;*
> *Though their voices are silent, their pleading looks will say,*
> *Oh! Hard times come again no more.*

Indeed, for Foster himself, hard times did come. Estranged from his wife and family, and despite having earned sizeable royalties, he died in penury at the age of 37 in a New York City hospital. Sadly, he had become alcoholic, selling his songs for the price of a drink. At the time of his death the sum of his assets was three pennies and 38 cents in Civil War script.

~

Hard Times

Baritone Ukulele

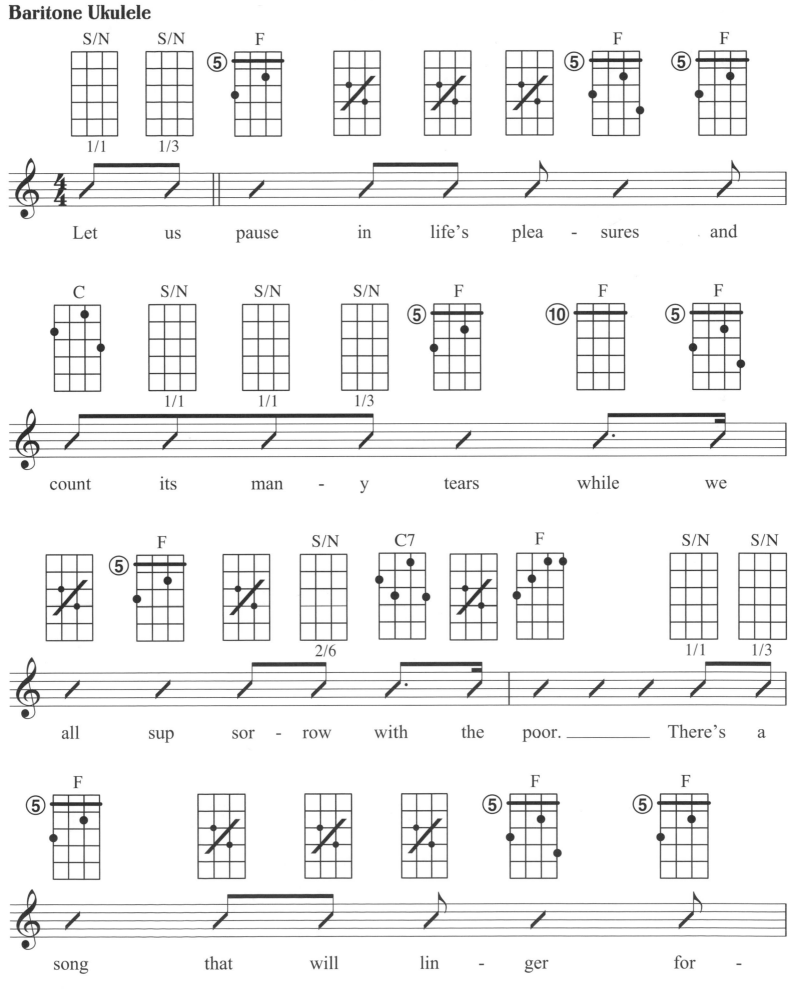

Let   us   pause   in   life's   plea - sures   and

count   its   man - y   tears   while   we

all   sup   sor - row   with   the   poor. _____ There's   a

song   that   will   lin - ger   for -

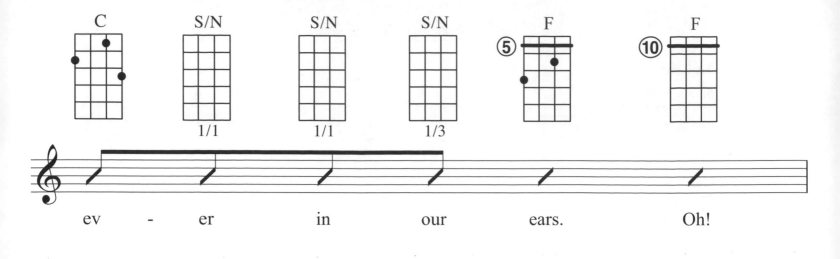

ev - er   in   our   ears.   Oh!

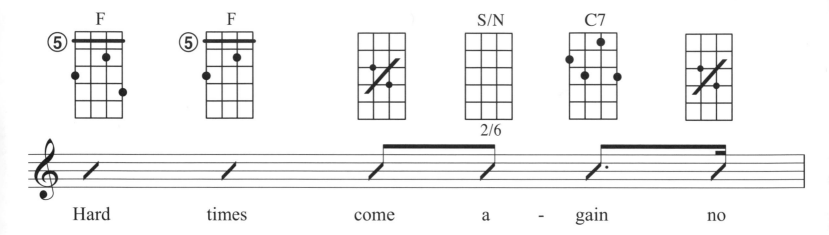

Hard   times   come   a - gain   no

Chorus

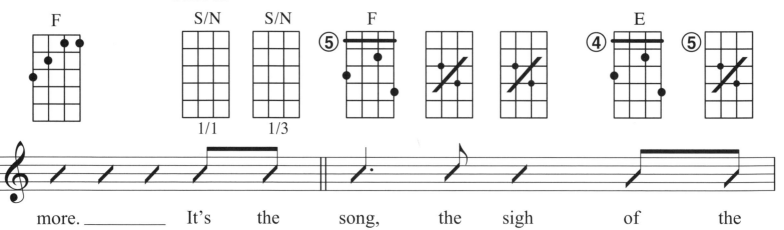

more. _____ It's   the   song,   the   sigh   of   the

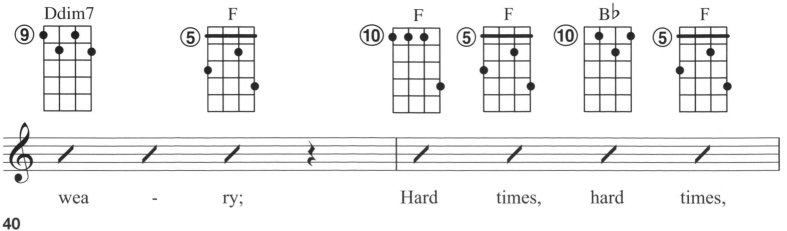

wea - ry;   Hard   times,   hard   times,

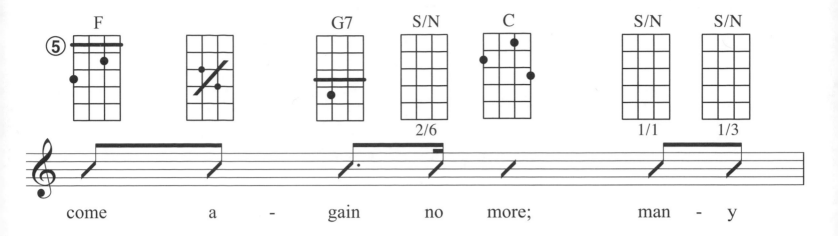

come   a -   gain   no   more;   man - y

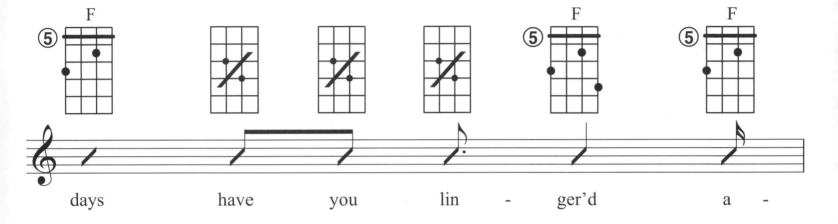

days   have   you   lin -   ger'd   a -

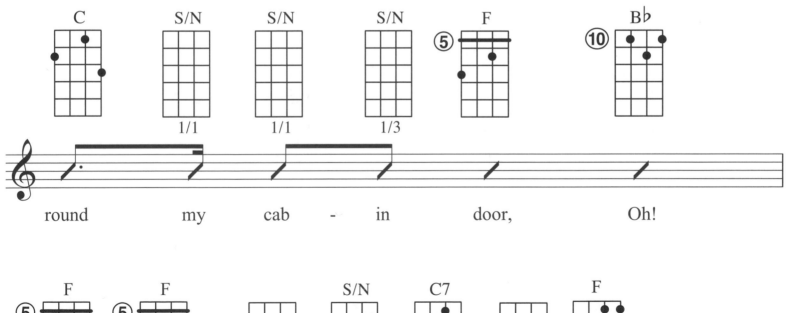

round   my   cab -   in   door,   Oh!

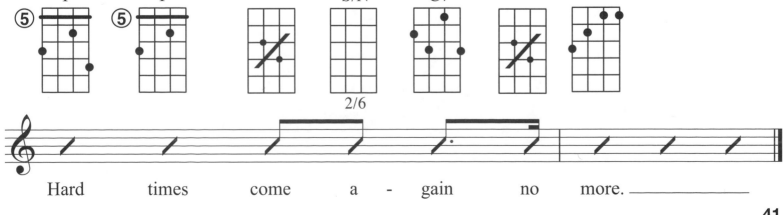

Hard   times   come   a -   gain   no   more. _____

HINE MA TOV

Traditional

Although one might expect to hear this Jewish melody played on an oud, or kinnor, or some other Middle Eastern instrument, it is certainly well suited to the rich sonorities of the ukulele.

The Hebrew text is from the Old Testament, the opening words of Psalm 133. Translated, the words are: "Behold, how good and how pleasant for brethren to dwell together in unity."

Possibly Syrian in origin, this hymn or chant is traditionally sung at special Shabbat services or as an Israeli folk song. Various melodies have been put to the words, but the version here appears to be the most common. The tune is uplifting and joyous, just as suitable for dancing and instrumental performance as for singing.

With the exception of one single note (2/3 found in the fifth measure), this arrangement uses single notes that are taken from the subsequent chord. Just form the chord and extract the single note before playing the chord.

Hine Ma Tov

Baritone Ukulele

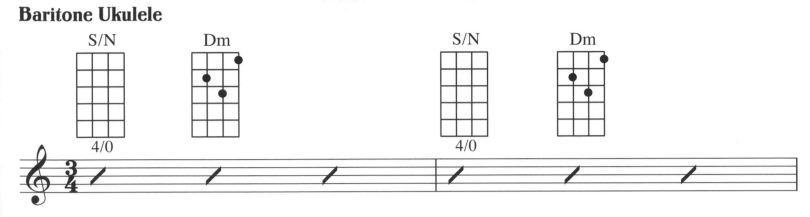

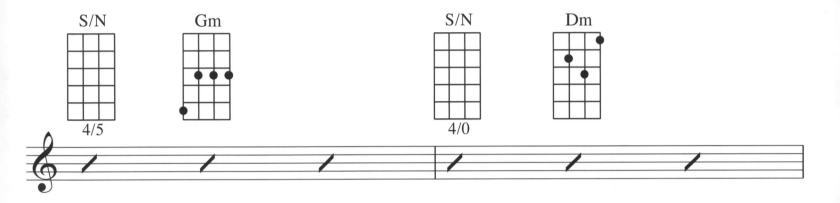

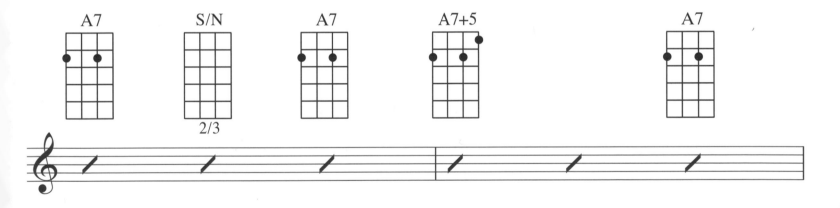

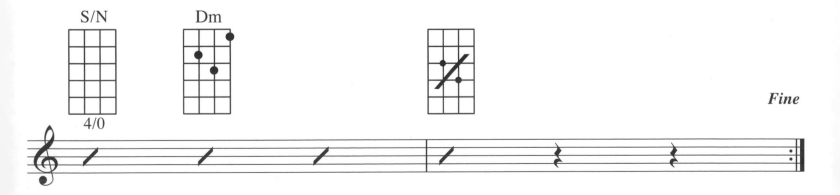

Fine

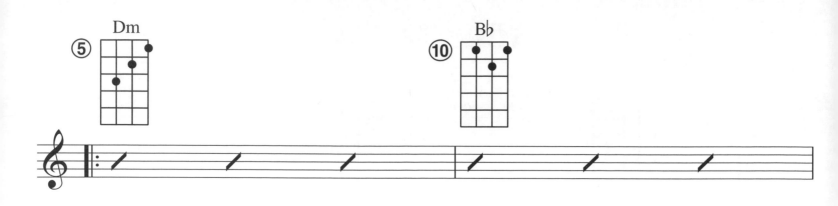

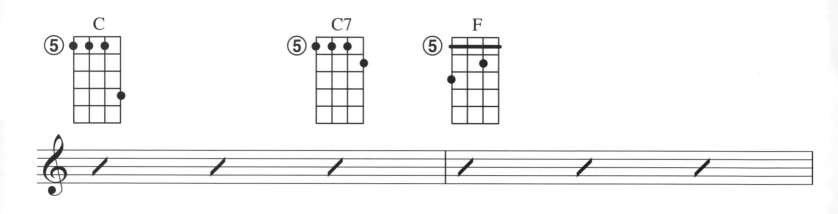

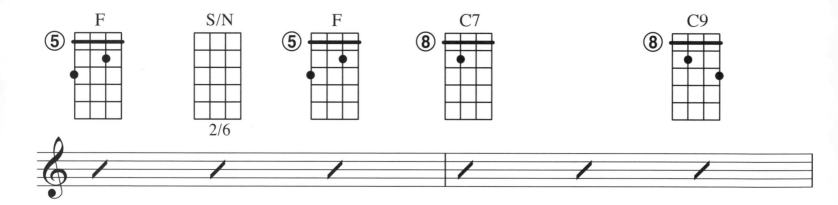

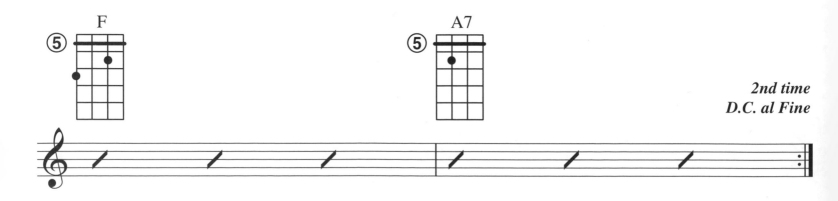

IN THE BLEAK MIDWINTER

(Circa 1906)

Words by CHRISTINA ROSSETTI

Music by GUSTAV HOLST

English born Christina Rossetti was a major poet of the Victorian 1800s. She was a deeply religious person with a dark, somber side to many of her poems. Despite the secular and seasonal feeling of the words included here, they are actually the first verse of a Christmas poem that has now become a popular carol. Four verses follow relating to the Christmas story, the last being almost as well known as the first:

> *What can I give Him,*
>
> *Poor as I am?*
>
> *If I were a shepherd*
>
> *I would bring a lamb.*
>
> *If I were a wise man*
>
> *I would do my part,*
>
> *Yet what I can I give Him –*
>
> *Give my heart.*

Gustav Holst was also from England, a prolific composer, instrumentalist, and teacher much influenced by simple English folk tunes. He is perhaps best known for his composition "The Planets." Ten years after Rossetti's death in 1894, her Christmas poem was published in a collection of poetic works, and Holst soon set the poem to music. In 1906 text and music appeared in *The English Hymnal,* which gave rise to its subsequent popularity as a Christmas carol.

In The Bleak Midwinter

Baritone Ukulele

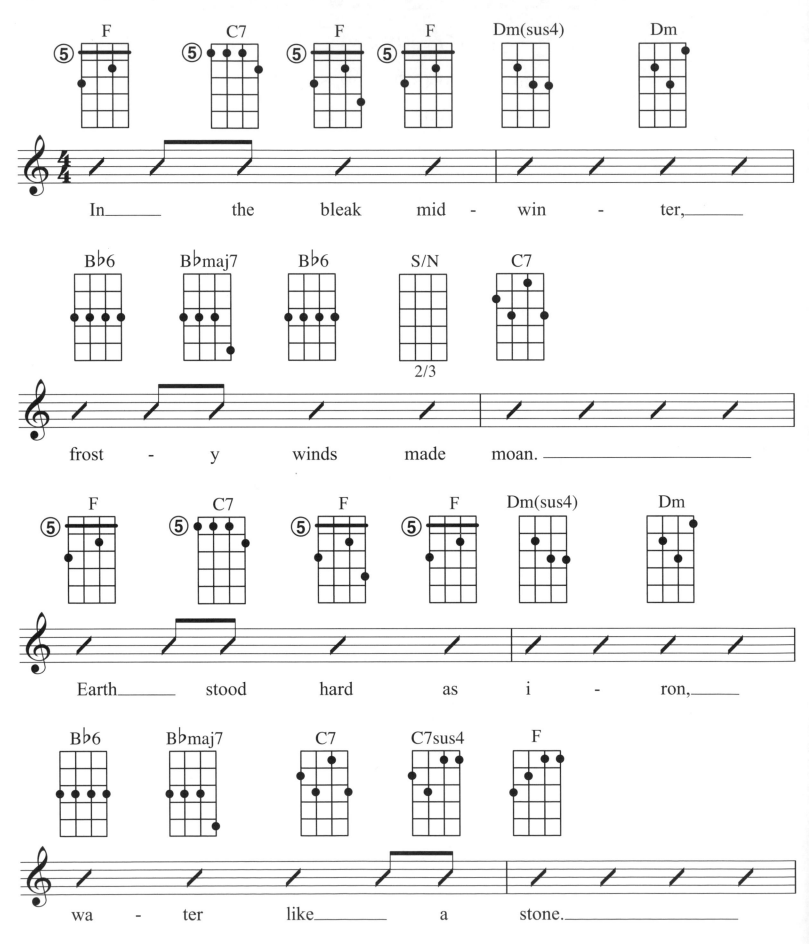

In_____ the bleak mid - win - ter,_____

frost - y winds made moan. _____

Earth_____ stood hard as i - ron,_____

wa - ter like_____ a stone. _____

JA-DA

(1918)

Words and Music by BOB CARLETON

Gents, get out your raccoon coat, brush the moth balls from your bell-bottom flannels and checkered knickers, unbuckle your galoshes, and dust off that porkpie hat for this favorite song of the Roaring '20s. Ladies, bob your hair, roll down your stockings, rouge your knees, and dig out that old cloche hat in the attic. Those crazy dances, the Charleston and Black Bottom, are back in style. And you, with your ukulele, why, you're the bee's knees, the cat's pajamas, the life of the party. It's 23 skidoo, Oh! you kid, and boop-boop-a-doop!

Cliff Edwards, also known as "Ukulele Ike" did much to popularize the song with Carleton on the vaudeville stage. Edwards was the voice of Jiminy Cricket in the Disney film *Pinocchio*, and sang the film's memorable version of "When You Wish Upon a Star." As his nickname suggests, he was a great exponent of the uke. He played a Martin ukulele, first the smaller version and subsequently, like Arthur Godfrey, the larger size tenor or baritone.

Cliff Edwards aka Ukulele Ike

Ja-Da

Baritone Ukulele

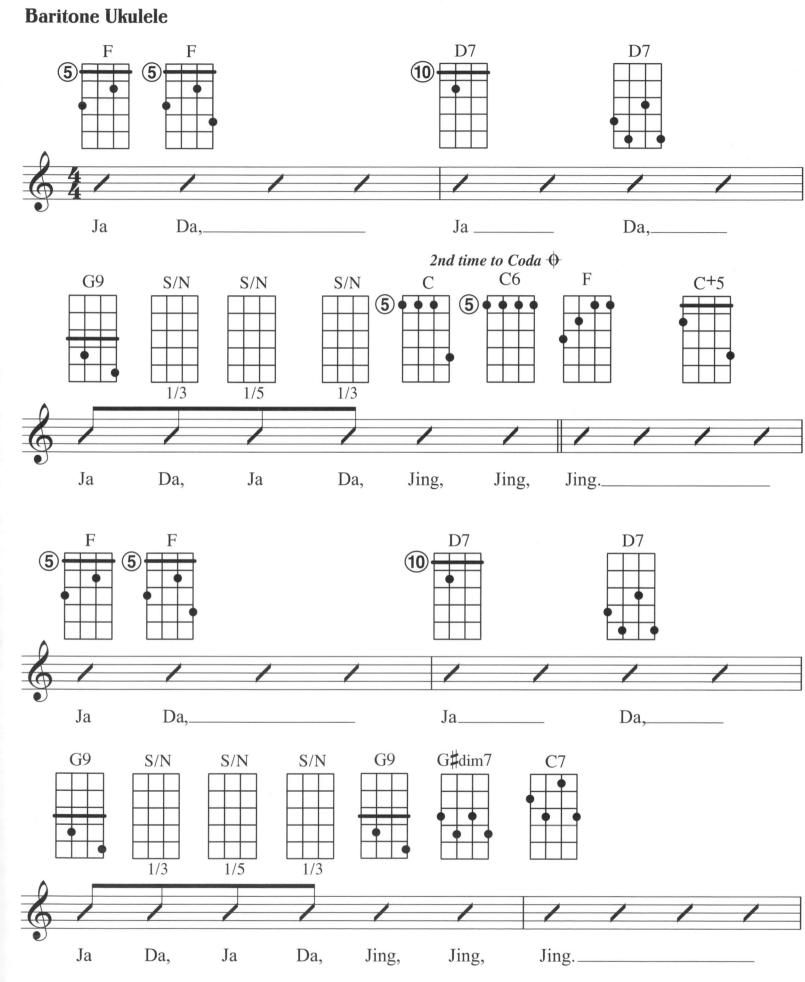

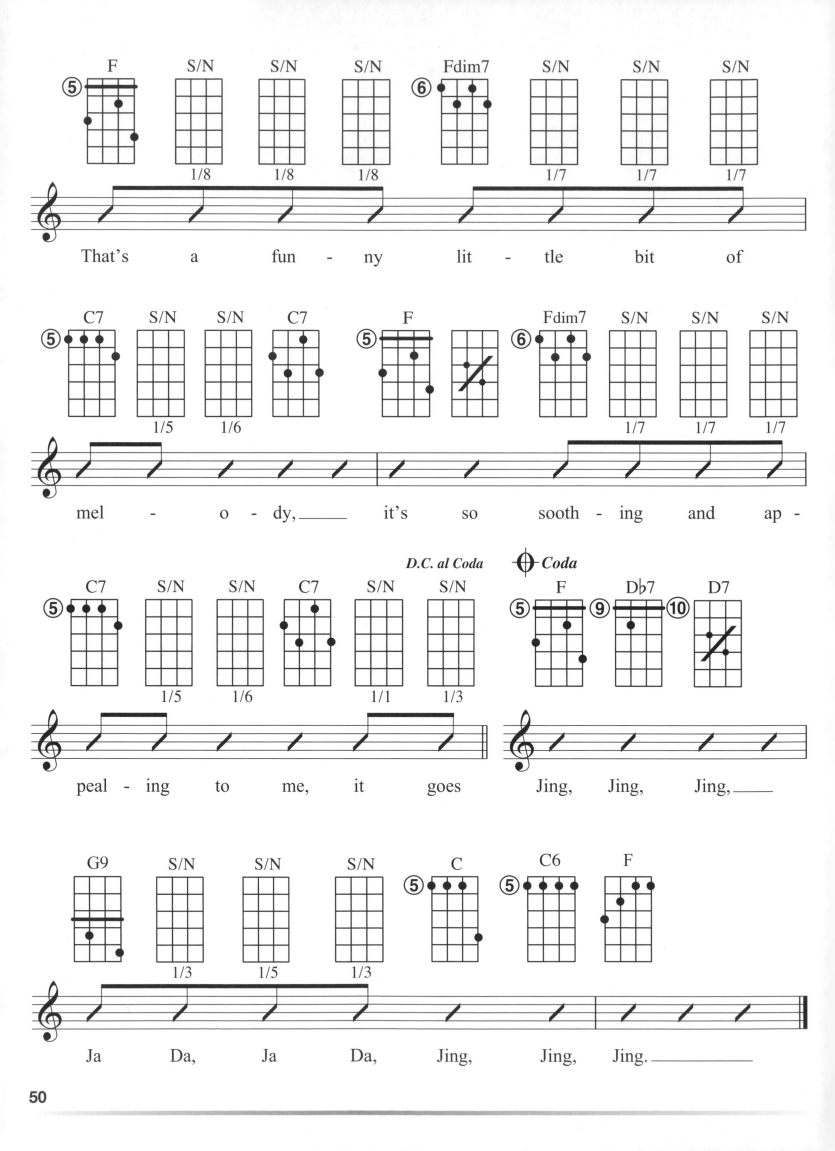

That's   a   fun - ny   lit - tle   bit   of

mel - o - dy,_____ it's   so   sooth - ing   and   ap -

peal - ing   to   me,   it   goes

Jing,   Jing,   Jing,_____

Ja   Da,   Ja   Da,   Jing,   Jing,   Jing._____

LIEBESTRAUM

(1850)

By FRANZ LISZT

One of a set of three piano solos, this is No. 3 and the most readily recognized. Translation of the German title is "Love Dream." It was popularized by plectrum banjo player Don Van Palta ("The Flying Dutchman") in the mid-1960s on the *Mickie Finn's* television show. Van Palta's virtuoso performance was visually enhanced by his wearing white gloves while playing on a darkened stage illuminated only by a black light. All that could be seen were the gloves, which appeared to be floating in air completely detached from a body.

A memorable movie moment comes from the 1959 film *Some Like It Hot*, with Tony Curtis, Jack Lemmon, and Marilyn Monroe. The scene is a dingy funeral parlor that acts as a front for a rip-roaring speakeasy hidden in back. Creating a diversionary sepulchral mood is a somber mortician seated at an organ playing a dirgeful rendition of—alas, you guessed it—"Liebestraum."

Liszt obviously had neither the banjo nor the ukulele in mind when he composed the piece and certainly not a funeral parlor. But, as you'll see, it makes a fine solo for a fretted instrument. The version in this collection is slightly abbreviated.

Liebestraum

Baritone Ukulele

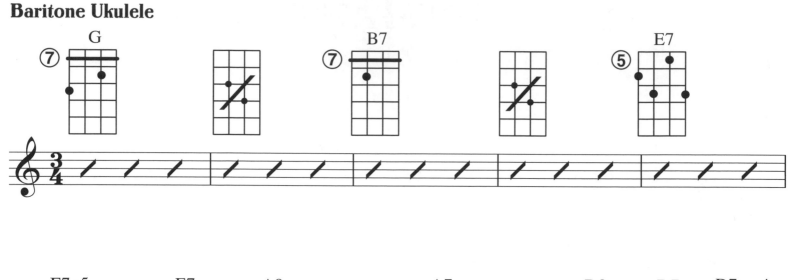

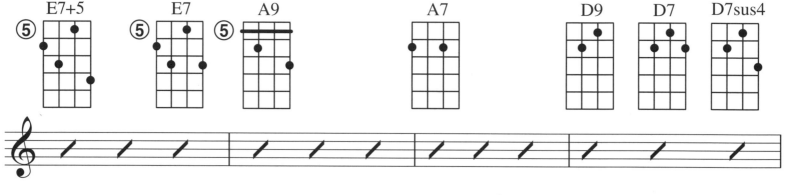

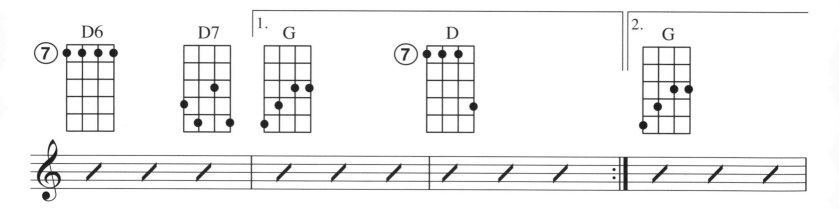

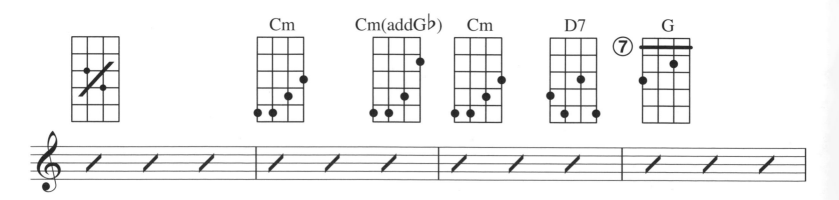

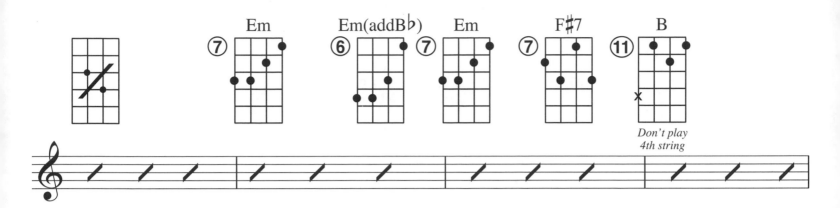

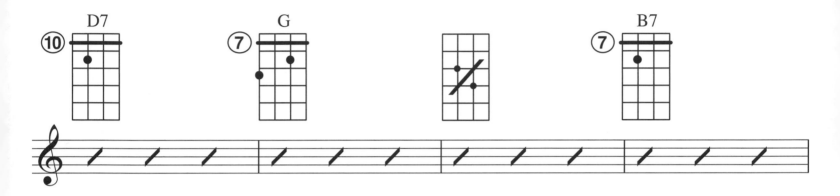

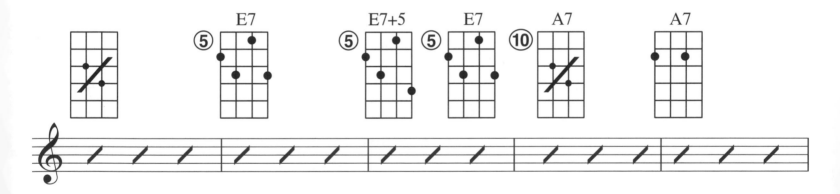

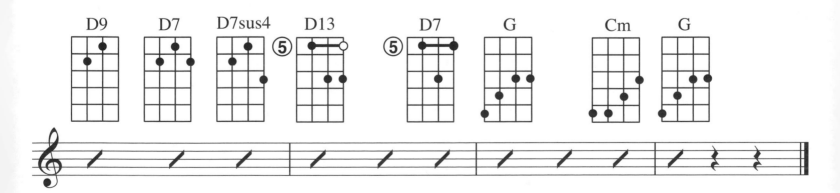

LOVE'S OLD SWEET SONG

(1884)

Words by G. CLIFTON BINGHAM
Music by JAMES L. MOLLOY

It is so easy to envision the family gathered around the parlor upright singing this sentimental favorite, or the neighborhood diva holding forth in recital with half-closed eyes, elbows flared, hands interlocked.

Librettist W.S. Gilbert (of Gilbert & Sullivan fame), songwriter Hoagy Carmichael, and classical composer Peter Ilyich Tchaikovsky all studied law, but abandoned the profession for the craft of making music. Composer James Malloy, a lawyer, was similarly inclined and embraced music as an avocational pursuit.

Conversely, lyricist Clifton Bingham's sole career was as a writer. He was an established author, drama critic, and poet especially noted for his verses in children's books. He claimed the words to "Love's Old Sweet Song" were the result of a pre-dawn early morning inspiration. How visual and apt his descriptive lyric phrase "When the flick'ring shadows, softly come and go …"

In 1911, two years prior to his death, Bingham published a novel with the same title as this song in which the narrator gives his new bride a copy of the song for a wedding present. It is said that "Love's Old Sweet Song" was a favorite of Malloy's fellow Irishmen, tenor John McCormack and James Joyce, the noted poet and author. Joyce was himself an amateur musician who made mention of the song in his novel Ulysses.

There's a verse in 4/4 time to "Love's Old Sweet Song" but only the chorus in 3/4 is presented here. Try playing it without strict adherence to tempo and note values. Tease and savor the chords, stretch them out in a free "rubato" manner.

Love's Old Sweet Song

Baritone Ukulele

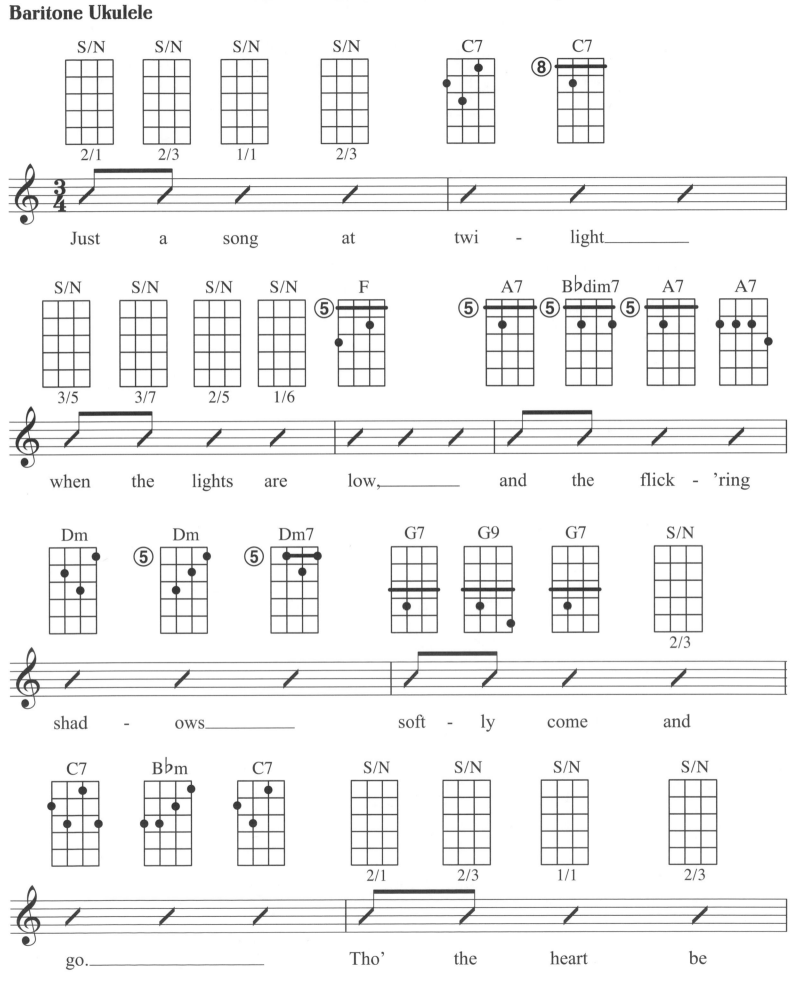

Just a song at twi - light_____

when the lights are low,_____ and the flick - 'ring

shad - ows_____ soft - ly come and

go._____ Tho' the heart be

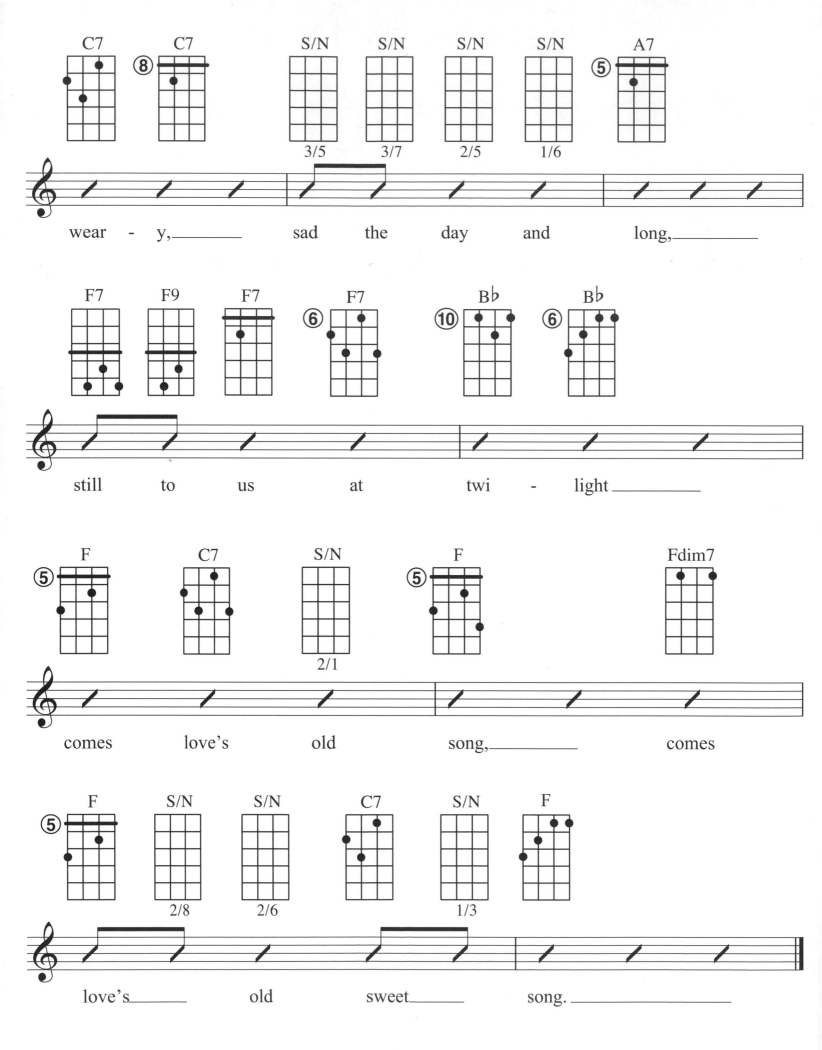

MEET ME TONIGHT IN DREAMLAND

(1909)

Words by MARY SLATER WHITSON
Music by LEO FRIEDMAN

Dreamland! That sentimental destination of reverie was also the name of a famous turn-of-the-century amusement park on Coney Island. Gents in derby hats and ladies with long skirts that skimmed the ground would ride the paddlewheel boats from Manhattan to the piers that would take them to a world of fantasy. Elegant architecture was ablaze with the novelty of a million electric lights. Sophisticated and cultural entertainment abounded offering a wonderland of sights to see and a variety of rides to enjoy. Further attractions were available at adjacent Luna Park and Steeplechase, while swimmers could opt to rent a bathing suit and splash in the ocean.

Tragically, after only seven years of operation, a devastating fire brought the end to Dreamland in 1911. Two years before, despite a sale of several million copies, the song brought little return to Whitson and Friedman who had sold it outright to a publisher who disliked paying royalties. The situation was reversed in 1910 with a different publisher and a new song by the talented team that sold over four million copies—"Let Me Call You Sweetheart."

Although Coney Island still exists as an amusement area, its glory days and those of Dreamland have faded to a memory. Fortunately the song, with its dual association of fanciful slumber and a Coney Island rendezvous, has survived and the memories preserved.

Meet Me Tonight In Dreamland

Baritone Ukulele

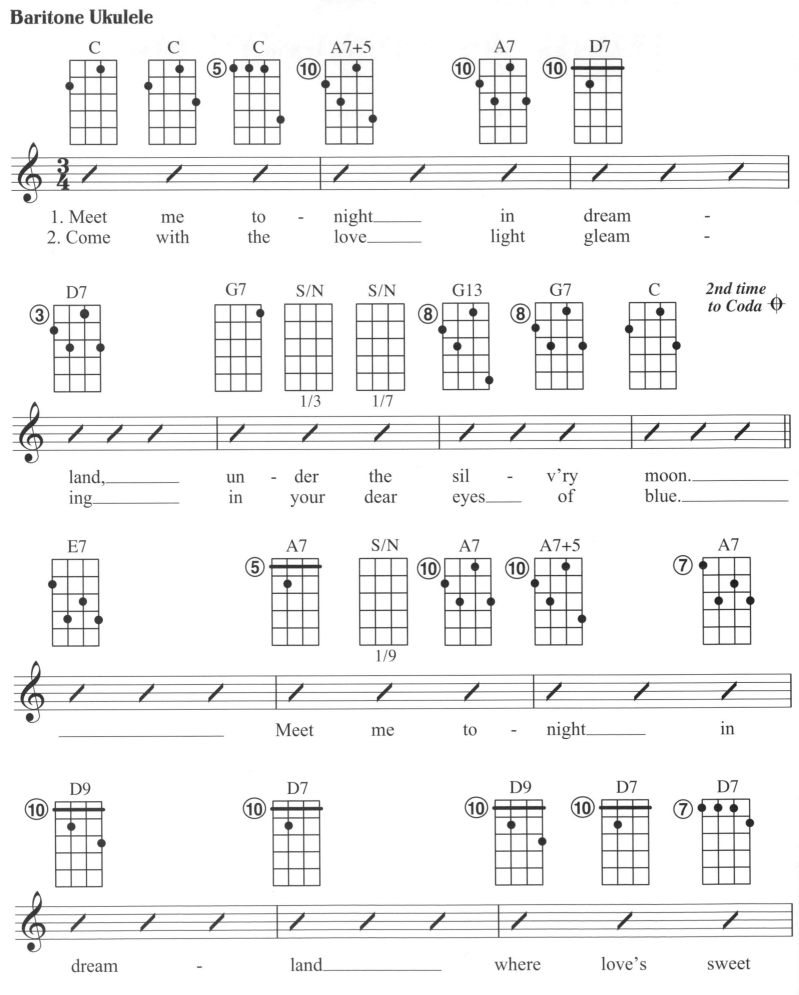

1. Meet me to - night_____ in dream -
2. Come with the love_____ light gleam -

land,_____ un - der the sil - v'ry moon.
ing_____ in your the dear eyes_____ of blue._____

2nd time to Coda

_____ Meet me to - night_____ in

dream - land_____ where love's sweet

58

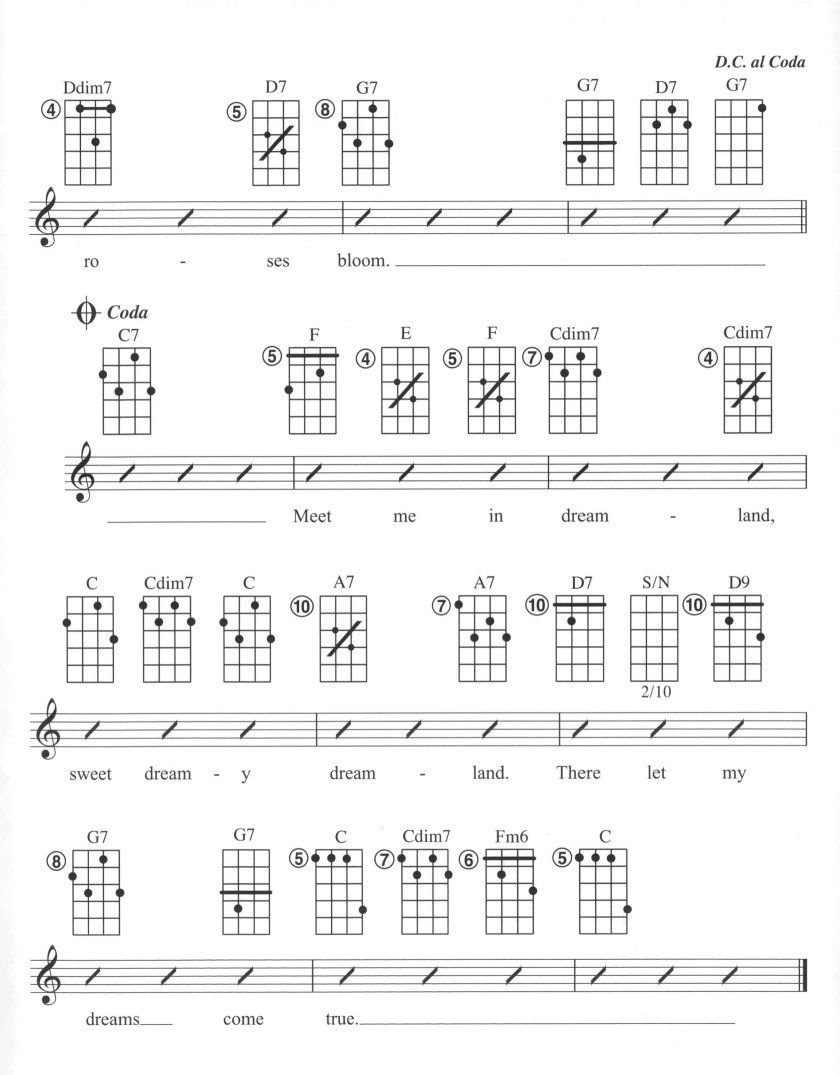

ro - ses bloom. _____

Coda

_____ Meet me in dream - land,

sweet dream - y dream - land. There let my

dreams___ come true._____

MELODY IN F

Opus 3, No. 1

(1852)

By ANTON RUBINSTEIN

One of the most popular pieces for the classical piano, especially in simplified form for beginning players, this graceful melody with its series of half-step drops adapts well to the ukulele. Rubinstein, a child prodigy, was born in Russia in 1829. He was a keyboard virtuoso who wrote extensively for the instrument including sonatas, serenades, and suites among other compositions. His enormous talent was acknowledged by such contemporary greats as Chopin, Liszt, and Mendelssohn. Rubinstein spoke four major languages and was literate in two more, a talent that certainly must have been useful as he toured Europe and America both performing and conducting.

In 1872, Rubinstein was engaged by the Steinway & Sons piano company to perform 200 concerts in the United States. Payment was $200 for each performance, paid in gold. The proceeds from this tour sustained him comfortably for the rest of his life. Anton Rubinstein should not be confused with Arthur Rubinstein, the well known Polish pianist of the 20th Century, who was no relation.

Playing tips: (1) Each of the first single notes in measures 1, 2, and 3 is contained in the chord that follows. (2) By muting the strings with an X, the melody is sustained. Playing those strings without the X is still harmonically correct. It's your choice to play them or not.

Melody in F

Baritone Ukulele

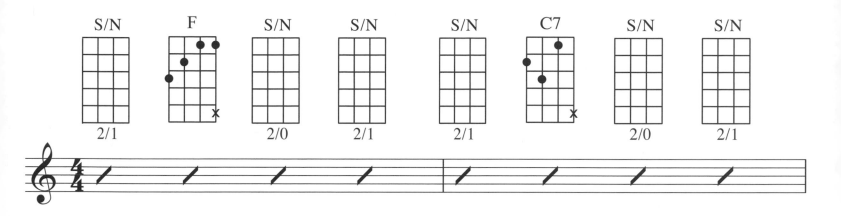

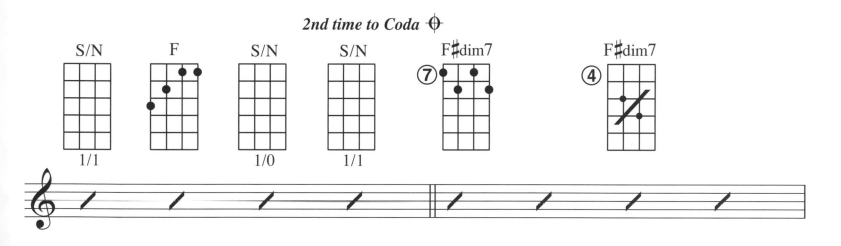

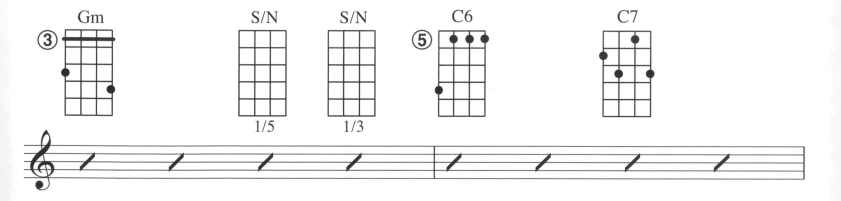

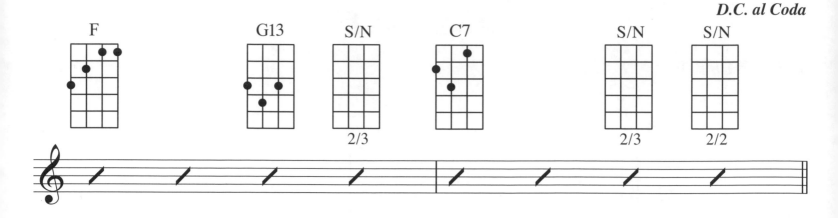

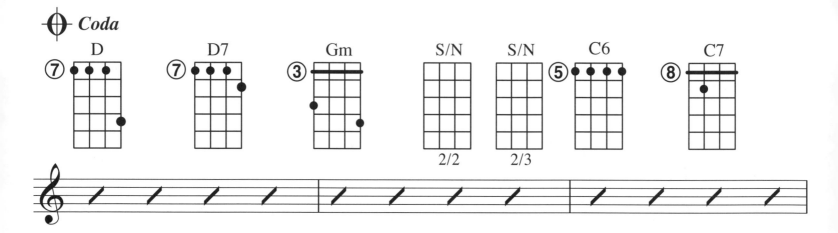

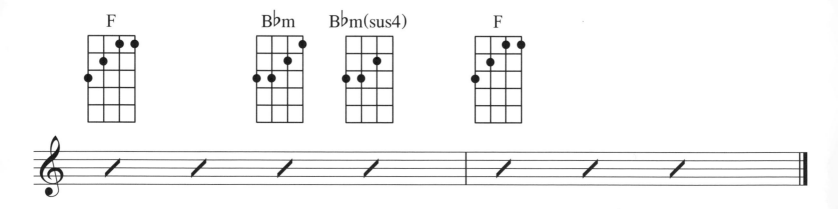

MEMORIES

(1915)

Words by GUS KAHN
Music by EGBERT A. VAN ALSTYNE

Before collaborating with Gus Kahn, Van Alstyne had already achieved success in 1905 with "In the Shade of the Old Apple Tree," written with Harry Williams. Over 700,000 sheet music copies were sold. The team of Van Alstyne and Williams had a long association that started with their days together touring in vaudeville before Van Alstyne became a song plugger, staff pianist, and composer of his own songs.

Van Alstyne began working with Gus Kahn after 1912. Their first hit was "Memories," a song that proved to be instantly popular with dance bands and continues to be an enduring favorite. The following year they are credited with writing the hit song "Pretty Baby," although there is some speculation that the melody was actually written by Tony Jackson, who allegedly sold the song for $250. On sheet music copies, Jackson is listed with Van Alstyne as a co-composer of the music.

Gus Kahn was probably the most prolific and successful lyricist of the first half of the 20th century. He was born in Germany, and it may have been that his immigrant background contributed to his finely tuned ear for language. From vaudeville to Broadway and on to Hollywood, his songs generated one hit after another. In addition to Van Alstyne, he collaborated with such greats as George and Ira Gershwin, Jerome Kern, Sigmund Romberg, and principally Walter Donaldson.

The catalog of well known songs with Kahn's lyrics seems endless. Among the many are "Carolina in the Morning," "Charley, My Boy," "Dream a Little Dream of Me," (popularized as a solo by Mama Cass Elliot of the '60s group The Mama & The Papas), "It Had to Be You," "Love Me or Leave Me," "Nobody's Sweetheart Now," "Makin' Whoopee," "Side by Side," "Yes Sir, That's My Baby," "Goofus," and with band leader Isham Jones, "I'll See You in My Dreams," which became the title of a movie based on Kahn's life.

Perhaps the most significant from our standpoint, were the lyrics to "Ukulele Lady." Sadly ironic that both Kahn and Van Alstyne were only inducted into the Songwriter's Hall Of Fame posthumously; Kahn some 30 years after his passing, Van Alstyne almost 20 years.

Memories

Baritone Ukulele

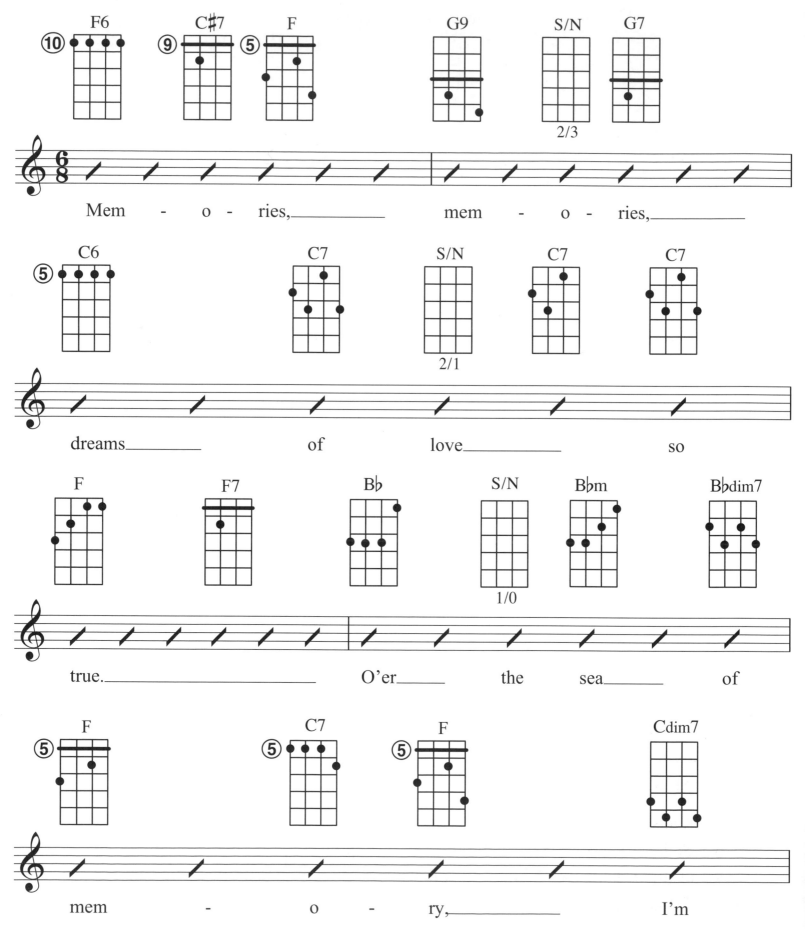

Mem - o - ries,_____ mem - o - ries,_____

dreams_____ of love_____ so

true._____ O'er_____ the sea_____ of

mem - o - ry,_____ I'm

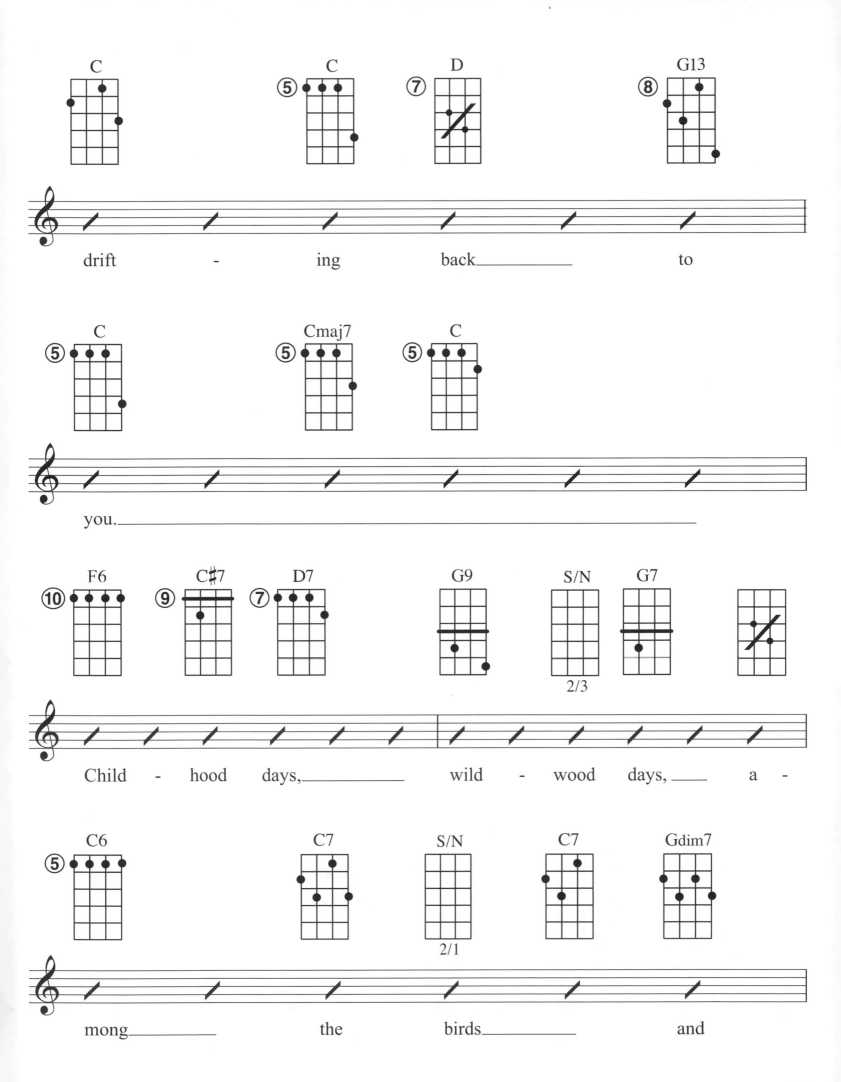

drift   -   ing   back_____   to

you._____

Child - hood days,_____   wild - wood days,_____   a -

mong_____   the   birds_____   and

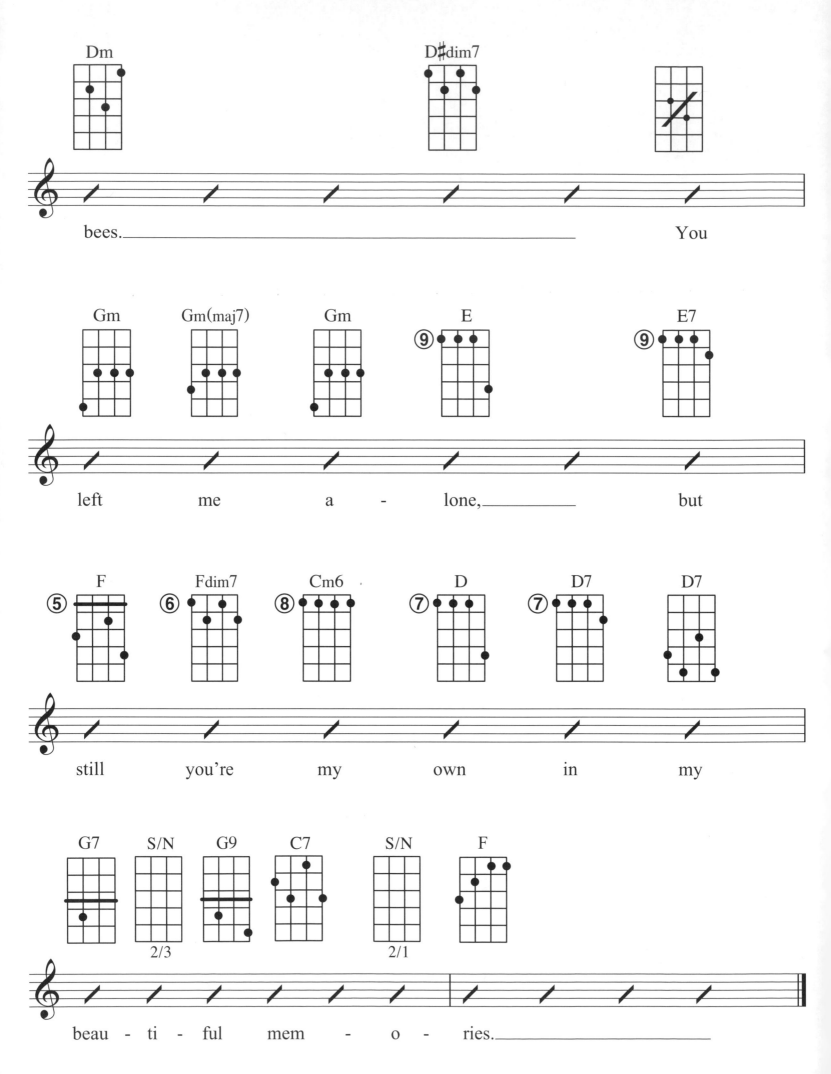

bees._____ You

left me a - lone,_____ but

still you're my own in my

beau - ti - ful mem - o - ries._____

MY BUDDY

(1922)

Words by GUS KAHN
Music by WALTER DONALDSON

Donaldson and Khan: a dream team of songwriting! Together and separately they produced a host of songs that skyrocketed into enormous popularity. One of Donaldson's first hit songs was written while he was serving and entertaining in World War I—"How Ya' Gonne Keep 'Em Down on the Farm." The Brooklyn son of a piano teacher, he himself was a pianist and songwriter for publishing houses along Tin Pan Alley, including that of the Irving Berlin Music Company. He later formed his own publishing firm, creating a long list of hits drawn from an output of over 600 songs. Among his many successes were "Little White Lies," "My Blue Heaven," and songs written with Kahn—"Carolina in the Morning," "Makin' Whoopee," "Love Me or Leave Me," and "Yes Sir, That's My Baby."

Before Al Jolson introduced "My Buddy" in 1922, there was another Donaldson hit for Jolson two years before, "My Mammy." It became a smash for Jolson who sang it in one of the first talking films, "The Jazz Singer" and later in the "Al Jolson Story." Jolson's rendition of "My Mammy" turned out to be one of the numbers most identified with him and a classic of songs about motherhood. His delivery style was often imitated, and just as often parodied.

It is interesting to note that at the time of composing a song about the Carolinas, Donaldson had never set foot in either one of those southern states. Ironic too that as an unmarried bachelor he should be linked with "My Blue Heaven" and its image of connubial contentment.

My Buddy

Baritone Ukulele

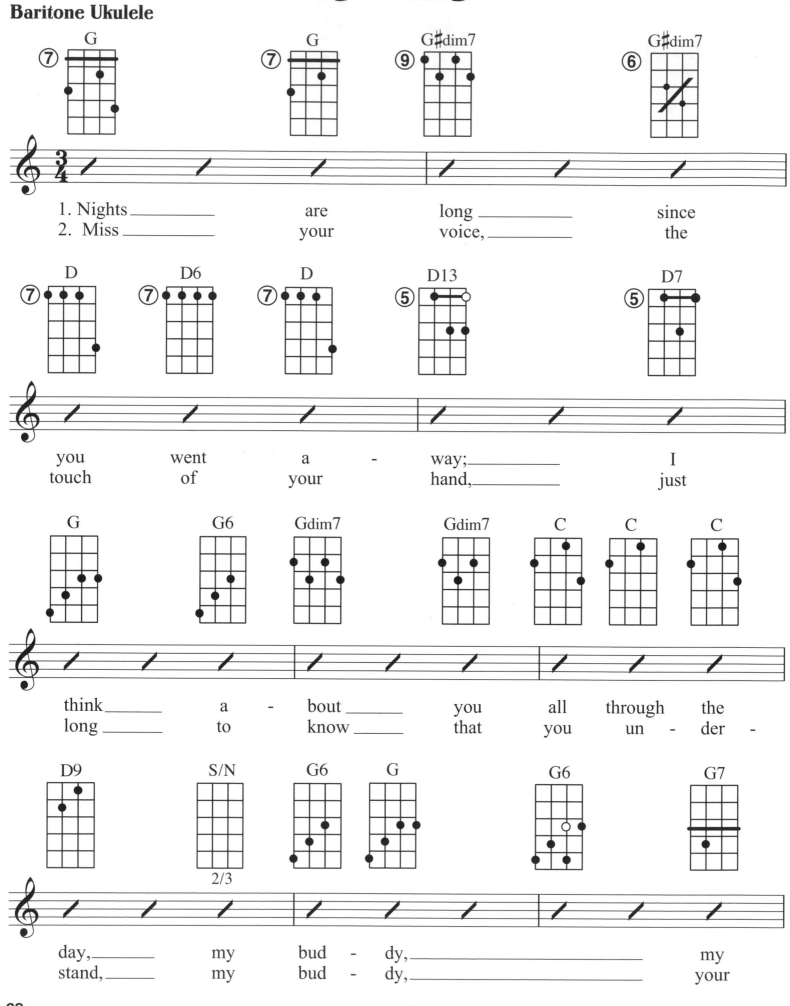

1. Nights _____ are long _____ since
2. Miss _____ your voice, _____ the

you went a - way; _____ I
touch of your hand, _____ just

think _____ a - bout _____ you all through the
long _____ to know _____ that you un - der -

day, _____ my bud - dy, _____ my
stand, _____ my bud - dy, _____ your

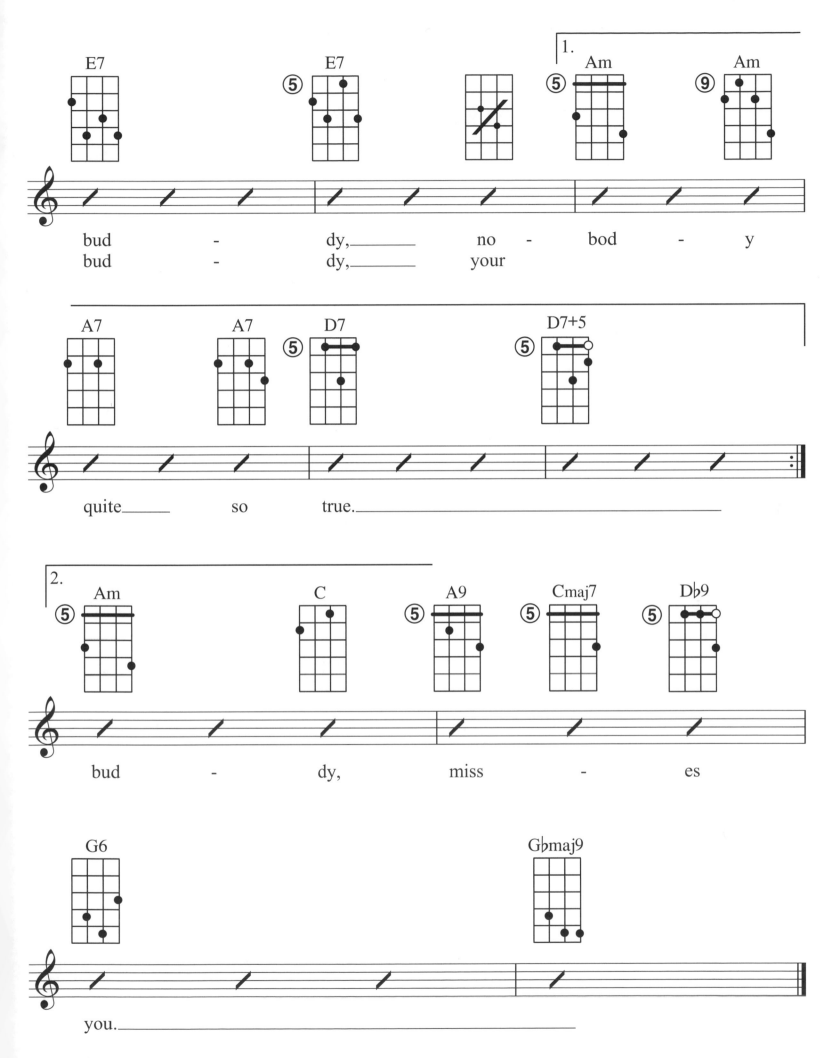

MY WILD IRISH ROSE

(1899)

Words and Music by CHAUNCEY OLCOTT

Although renowned for performance of Irish ballads and for acting in productions with nostalgic links to Ireland, it is interesting to note that Chancellor "Chauncey" Olcott was born not in Ireland but rather in Buffalo in upstate New York. His heritage, however, was Irish, and he identified with his ancestral roots in a show business career that spanned some 30 years.

Chauncey's background ranged from minstrel shows and operetta to touring theater groups that traveled extensively in this country and Europe. Combining talents as a lyric tenor, composer, and actor, he produced many original plays, comedies, and musicals, almost all with an Irish theme. Not surprising, he found receptive audiences at the turn of the century with newly arrived Irish immigrants, and indeed his songs continue to resonate today with those of Hibernian heritage. According to Chauncey's wife, a flower given to her by a child when the couple was visiting Ireland inspired this song. Asked the name of the flower, the reply was "It's a wild Irish rose." Credited with many original songs, lyrics, and collaborations, Chauncey is also especially noted for having written the words to "When Irish Eyes Are Smiling."

Despite his long-term Irish connection, it is somewhat ironic that Chauncey retired to Monte Carlo in France where he passed away in 1932 at age 73. His funeral was held in New York City at St. Patrick's Cathedral. Honorary pallbearers included Governor Alfred E. Smith, Mayor Jimmy Walker, and George M. Cohan.

My Wild Irish Rose

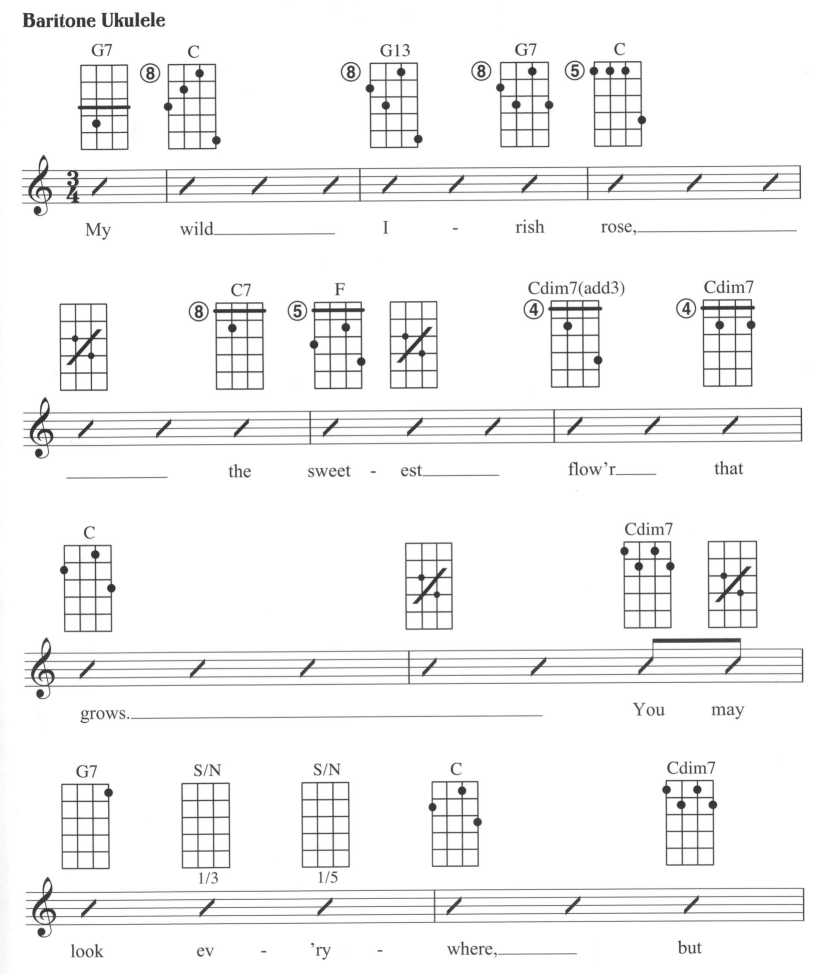

Baritone Ukulele

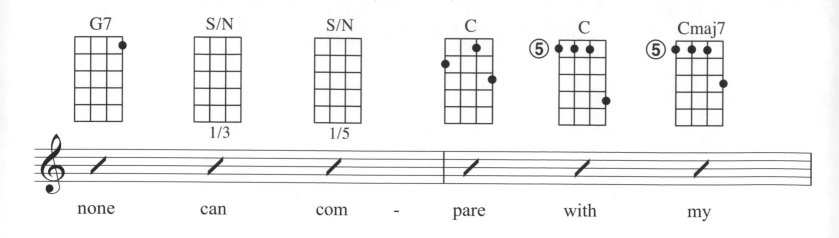

none can com - pare with my

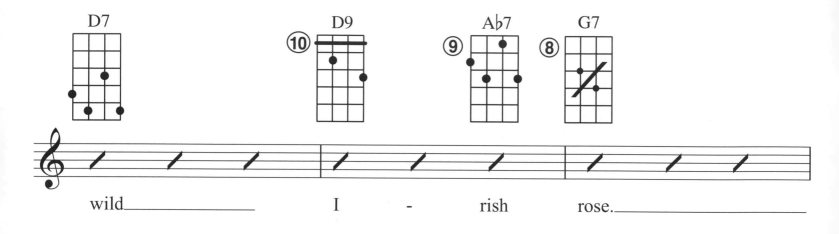

wild_____ I - rish rose._____

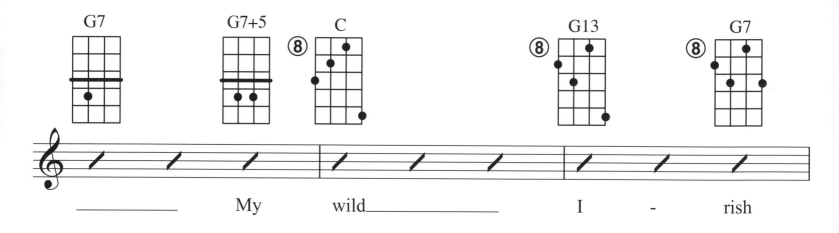

_____ My wild_____ I - rish

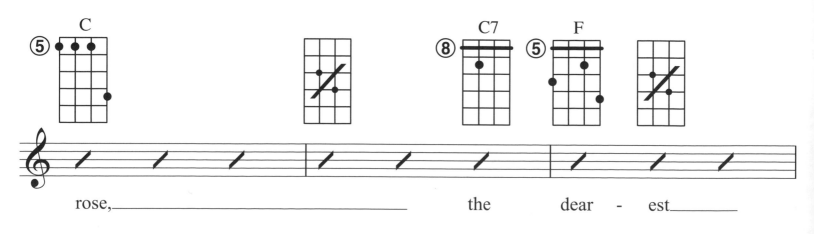

rose,_____ the dear - est_____

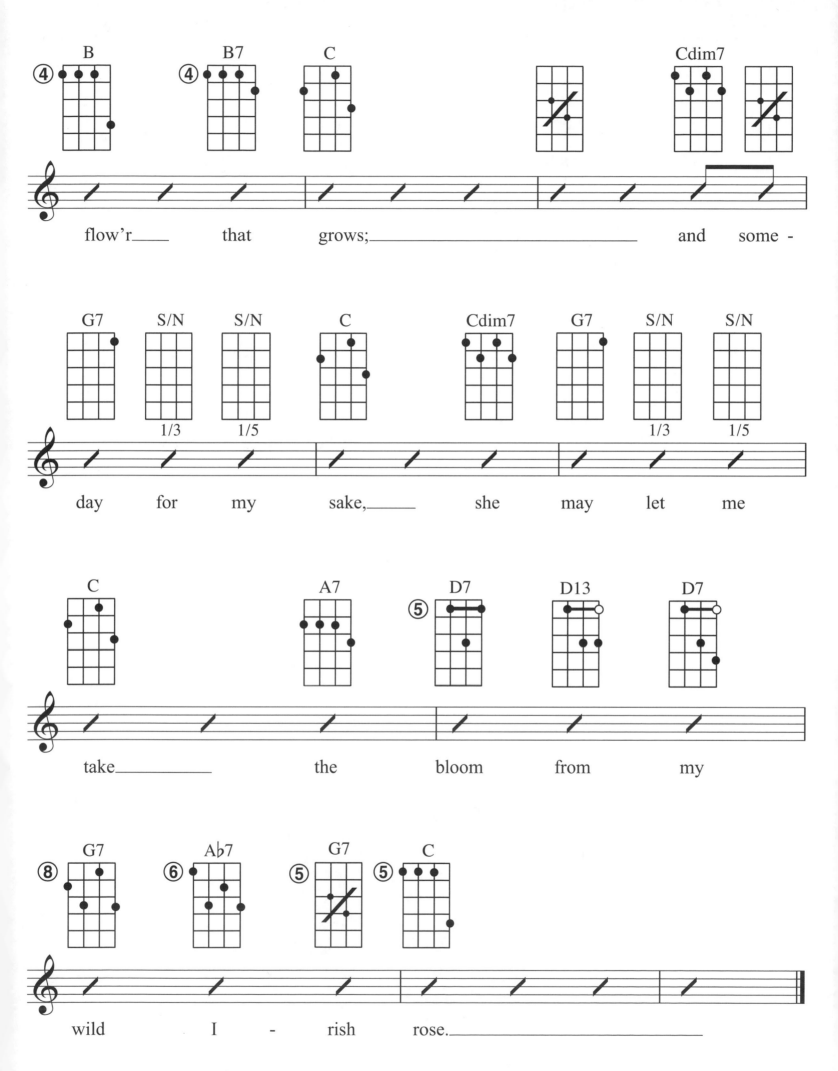

flow'r_____ that grows;_____ and some -

day for my sake,_____ she may let me

take_____ the bloom from my

wild I - rish rose._____

SOMEBODY STOLE MY GAL

(1918)

Words and Music by LEO WOOD

This song has come a long way since its introduction in 1918. Originally listed in recording company catalogs as a ragtime number, it has since been played in virtually all styles by a seemingly endless variety of bands and parade of singers. Jug bands, Dixieland bands (Kid Ory, Bix Beiderbecke), mummers string bands, barbershop groups, piano rolls—the song appears to be everywhere. Recordings range from the '20s (Ted Weems, Fletcher Henderson), through the '30s (Cab Calloway, Fats Waller), into the '40s (Count Basie, Benny Goodman), and right up to more recent times (Chet Atkins, Bobby Darin, Errol Garner, Merle Travis, Mitch Miller, and many others). Composer Leo Wood, who wrote for vaudeville and Broadway musicals, is perhaps best known for this song, but he is well remembered too for such popular classics as "Runnin' Wild," "Cherie," and "Wang Wang Blues," which is also included in this collection of ukulele solos.

Somebody Stole My Gal

Baritone Ukulele

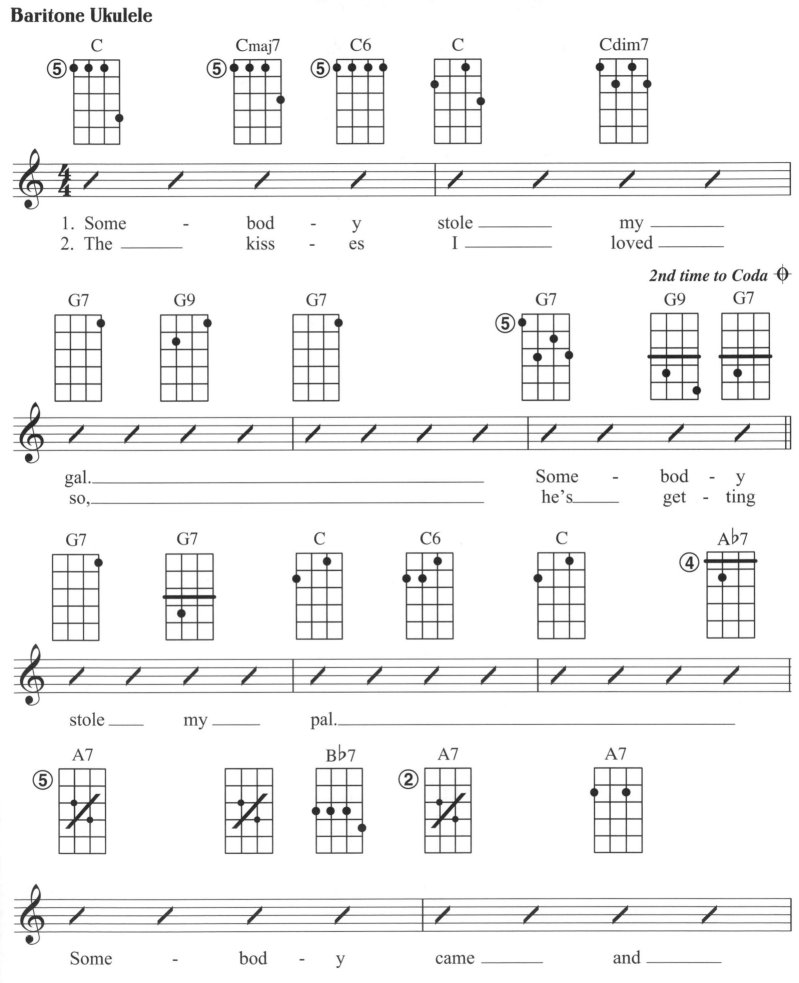

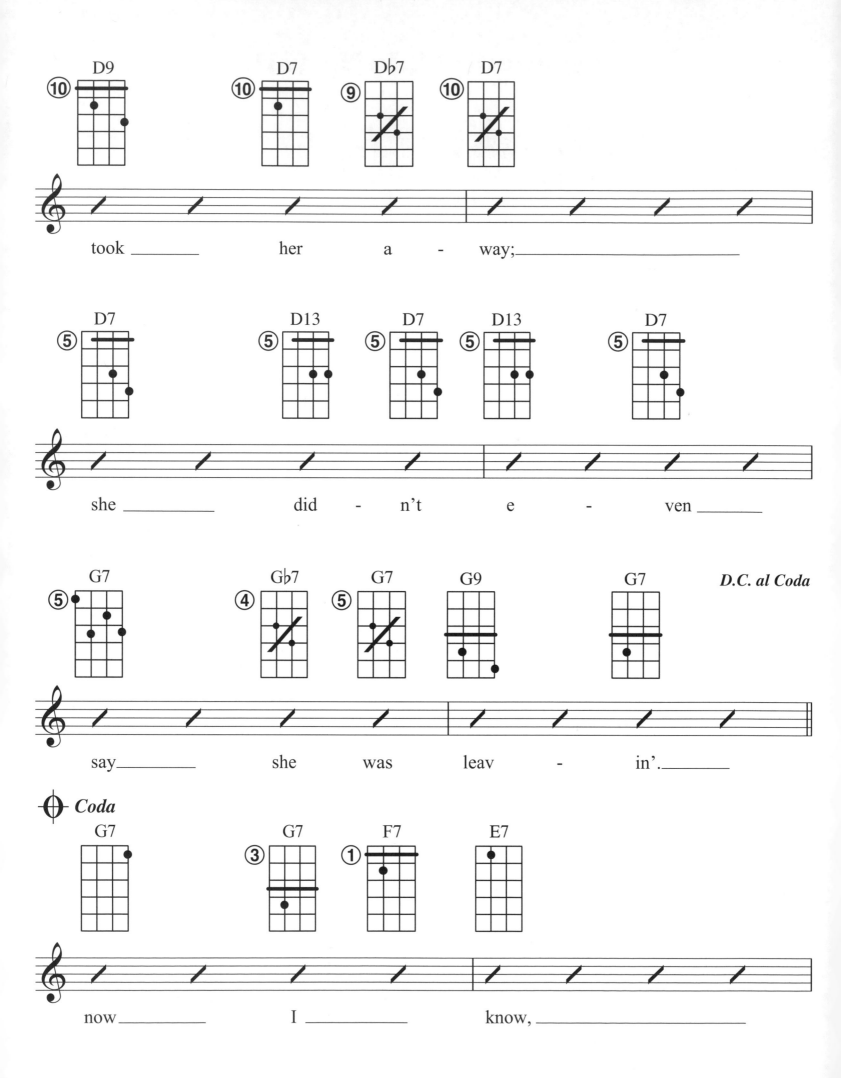

took _____ her a - way;_____

she _____ did - n't e - ven _____

say_____ she was leav - in'._____

D.C. al Coda

Coda

now_____ I _____ know, _____

76

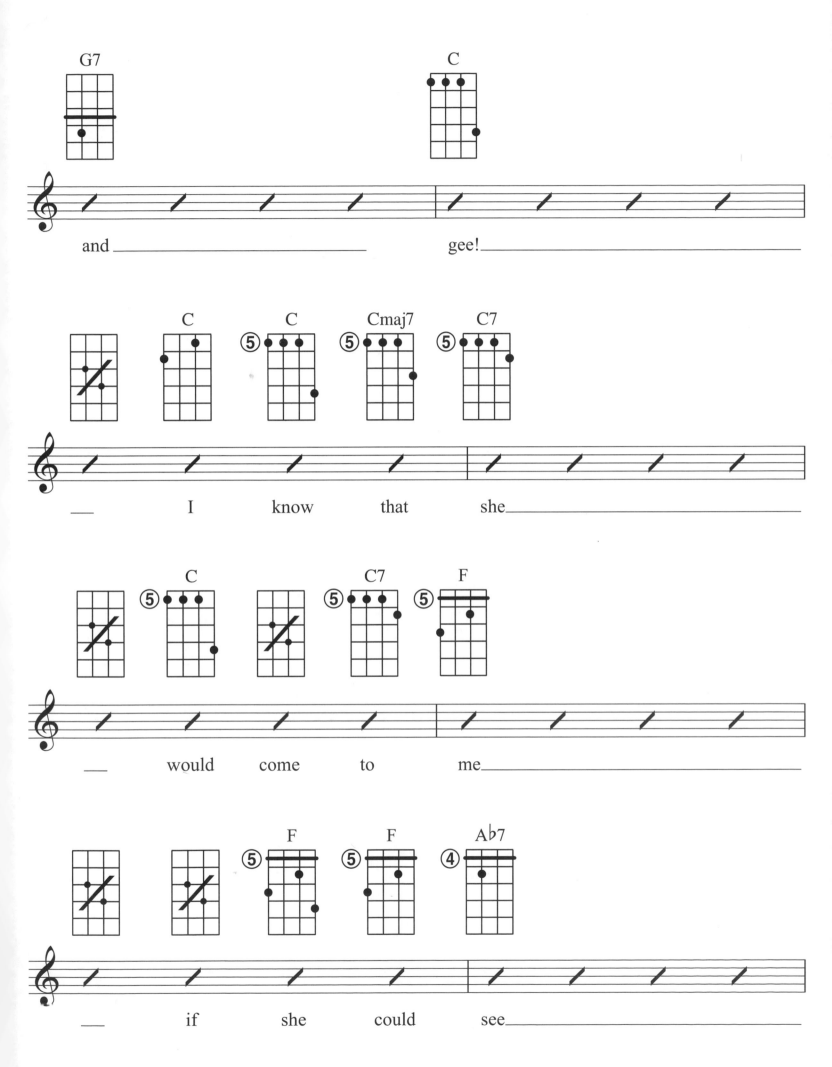

and _____ gee! _____

___ I know that she _____

___ would come to me _____

___ if she could see _____

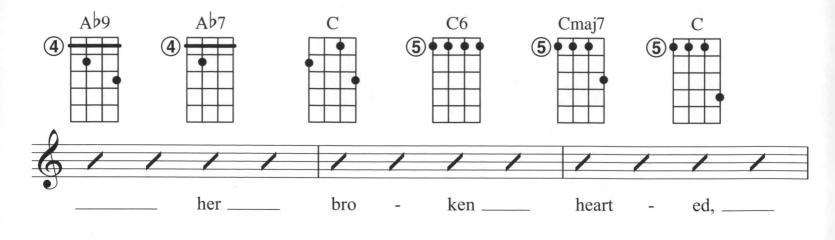

_____ her _____ bro - ken _____ heart - ed, _____

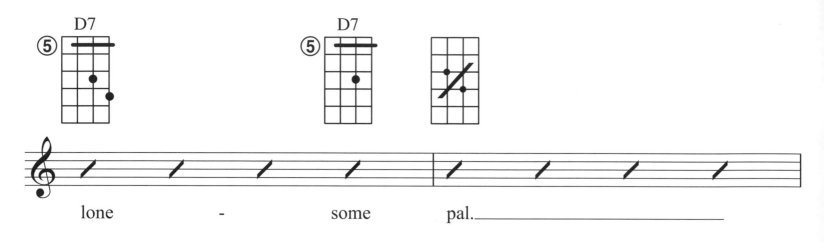

lone - some pal._____

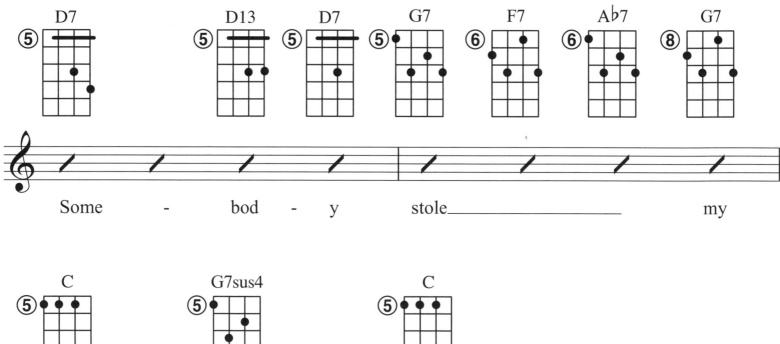

Some - bod - y stole_____ my

gal._____

STAGOLEE BLUES

Traditional

To the best of my knowledge there are no words for the version of the tune included in this collection. Its easy-going flow of chords and melody disguises the nature of the man whose name is in the title. Who was Stagolee? According to folk sources he was the equivalent of Jim Croce's "Bad, Bad Leroy Brown," that daunting character from the top-of-the charts hit in 1973. Legend has it that on Christmas Eve in 1895 one Lee Shelton, known as "Stag Lee" shot and killed Billy Lyons in a saloon squabble over a Stetson hat that Billy had taken from Stag.

Varying accounts of the murder, both mythical and real, took hold. Numerous versions were set to music under such titles as "Stag-A-Lee," "Stagger Lee," and "Stag-O'-Lee"—and these are only a few of the variants.

The first known recording of one song version was by Fred Waring's Pennsylvanians in 1923. Since then hundreds of artists have recorded the song, among them Duke Ellington, Fats Domino, and Elvis Presley. And the recordings have continued right up to the present day having taken on every imaginable form from blues, jazz, folk balladry, and even ragtime.

Just for reference, here's one verse as sung by Mississippi John Hurt:

"Gentlemens of the jury, whatch-you think of that?
Stagolee killed Billy Lyons 'bout a five-dollar Stetson hat."
That bad man, O cruel Stagolee.

Stagolee Blues

Baritone Ukulele

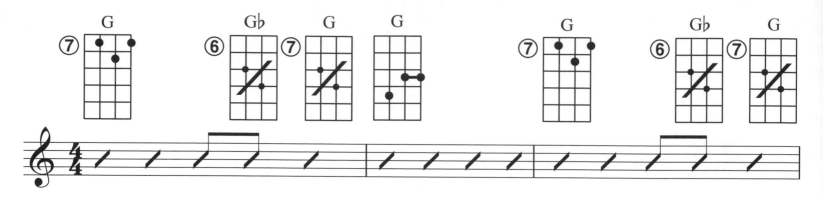

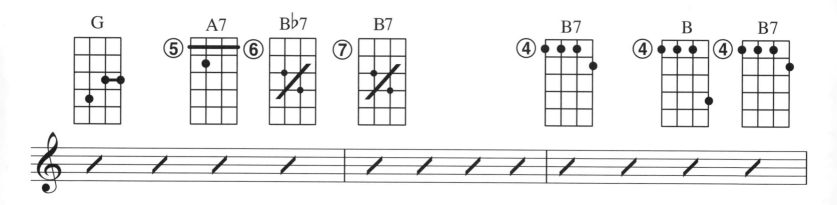

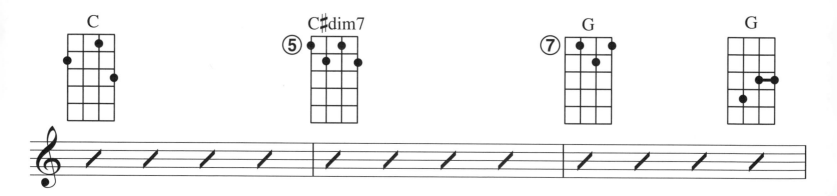

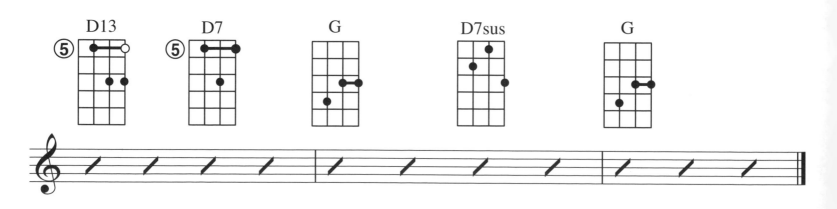

SWEET ADELINE

(1903)

Words by RICHARD H. GERARD
Music by HARRY ARMSTRONG

For over one hundred years, this song has remained a barbershop classic. A favorite of both organized and impromptu quartets, it is also a chorus standard regularly included in concert programs and barbershop competitions. The song's title was used for a 1929 musical by Hammerstein and Kern, later for a 1934 film based on the Broadway show. So popular is the song, with its potential for tight harmonies and echoed phrases, that its title has been adopted by the international group of lady barbershoppers, the Sweet Adelines.

Supposedly, a music clerk from a New York department store was the inspiration for the lyrics. But it wasn't until the title was changed from "You're the Flower of My Heart, Sweet Rosalie" that a publisher could be found. A billboard promoting the tour by a diva soprano, Adelina Patti, prompted the name switch, and as they say, the rest is history.

Sweet Adeline

Baritone Ukulele

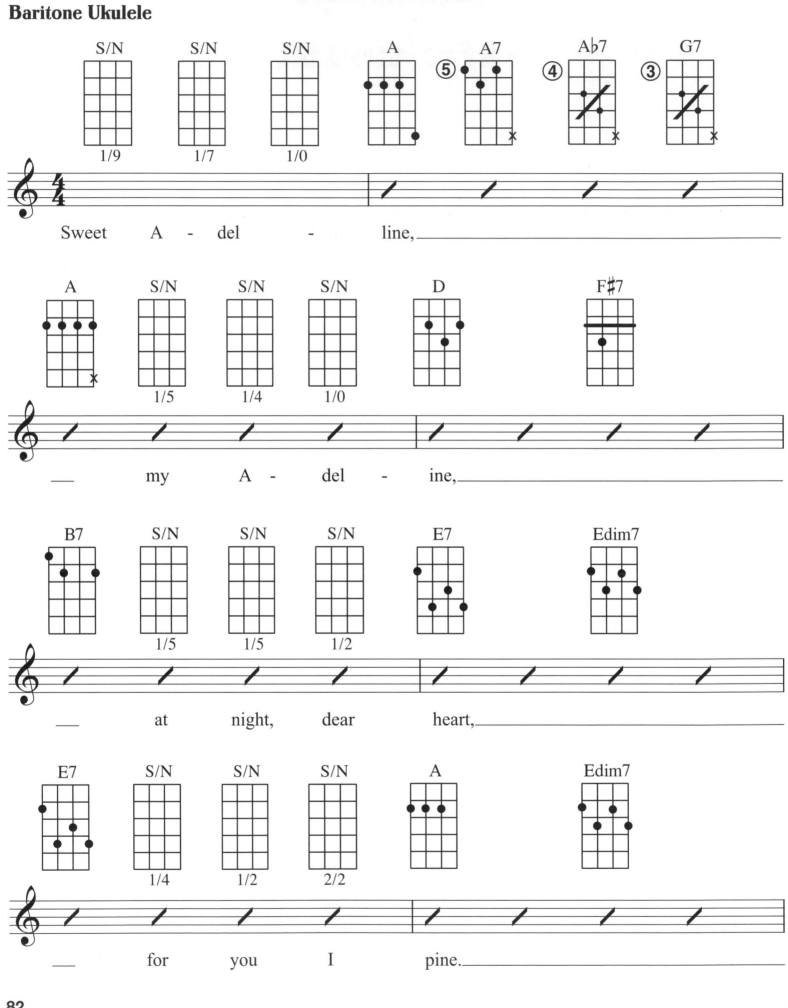

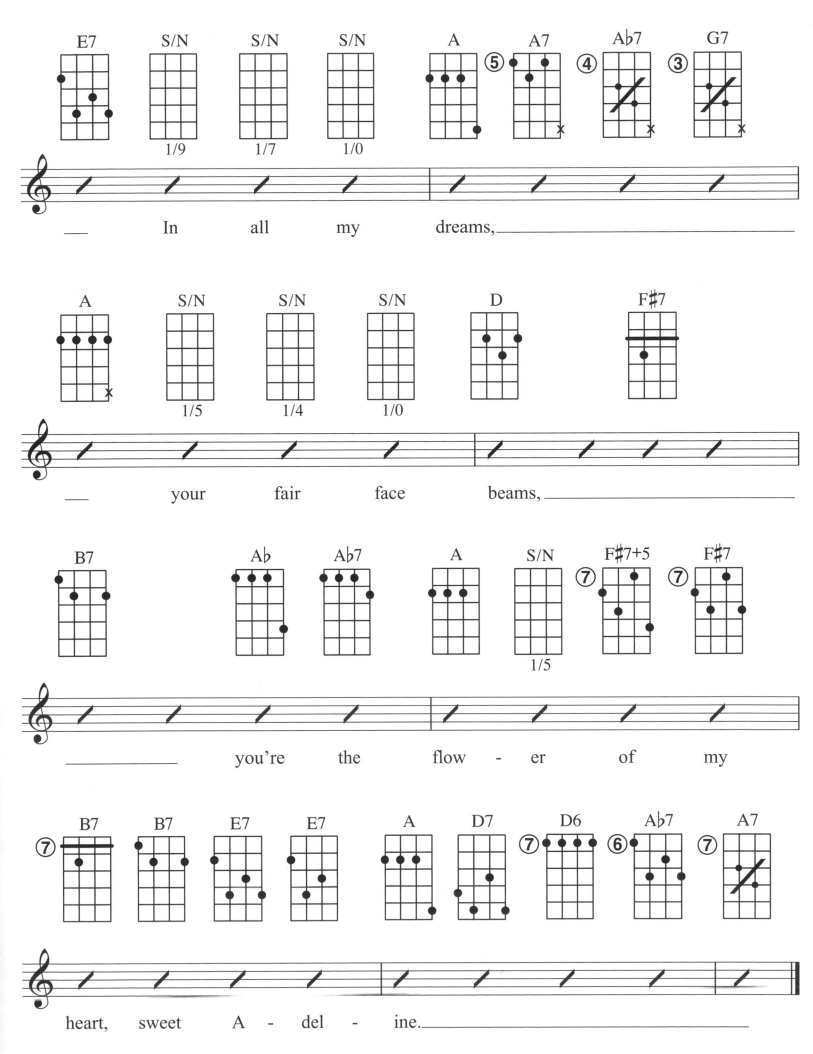

In all my dreams,

your fair face beams,

you're the flow - er of my

heart, sweet A - del - ine.

TOYLAND

(1903)

Words by GLEN MacDONOUGH
Music by VICTOR HERBERT

Babes in Toyland is one of Victor Herbert's most famous operettas, and the song "Toyland" is one of its noteworthy themes. The original production, along with many stage revivals, film versions, and numerous sound recordings, have been perennial favorites of the Christmas season for over one hundred years.

The operetta's somewhat dark and complicated plot follows a brother and sister who run away from home, and after being shipwrecked, find refuge in a mystical land of animated toys, villains, and a cast of dazzling costumed characters taken from the nursery rhymes of *Mother Goose.*

Possibly inspired by the song, a well known illustration by Maxfield Parrish depicts two colorful toy-like soldiers with muskets and crossed bandoleers standing guard at the entrance of a towering complex of medieval castles. Entitled "Toyland," the illustration appeared in 1908 on the cover of a Christmas edition of *Collier's* magazine. Offered by the magazine as an art print and also used as a poster for the Toy Show and Christmas Present Bazaar that same year, it was previously published in 1907 as the cover of a children's book.

The last eight measures of the "Toyland" melody were used in the 1950s for a popular radio jingle for Lustre-Creme shampoo. Magazine ads also promoted the product with endorsements by numerous Hollywood actresses like Marilyn Monroe, Doris Day, and Bette Davis. The jingle words were: "Dream Girl, Dream Girl, Beautiful Lustre-Creme Girl. You'll owe your crowning glory to a Lustre-Creme shampoo."

Playing Note: The single notes (3/7) in the concluding measures are contained in the Gm chords that follow. The second B♭m6 is easily played from the preceding C7 chord by just raising the 2nd and 4th strings one fret. The F6 and F chords in measure 5 contain the melody on the 2nd string, but there is no need to eliminate or mute the 1st string. The melody will come through playing all four strings.

Toyland

Baritone Ukulele

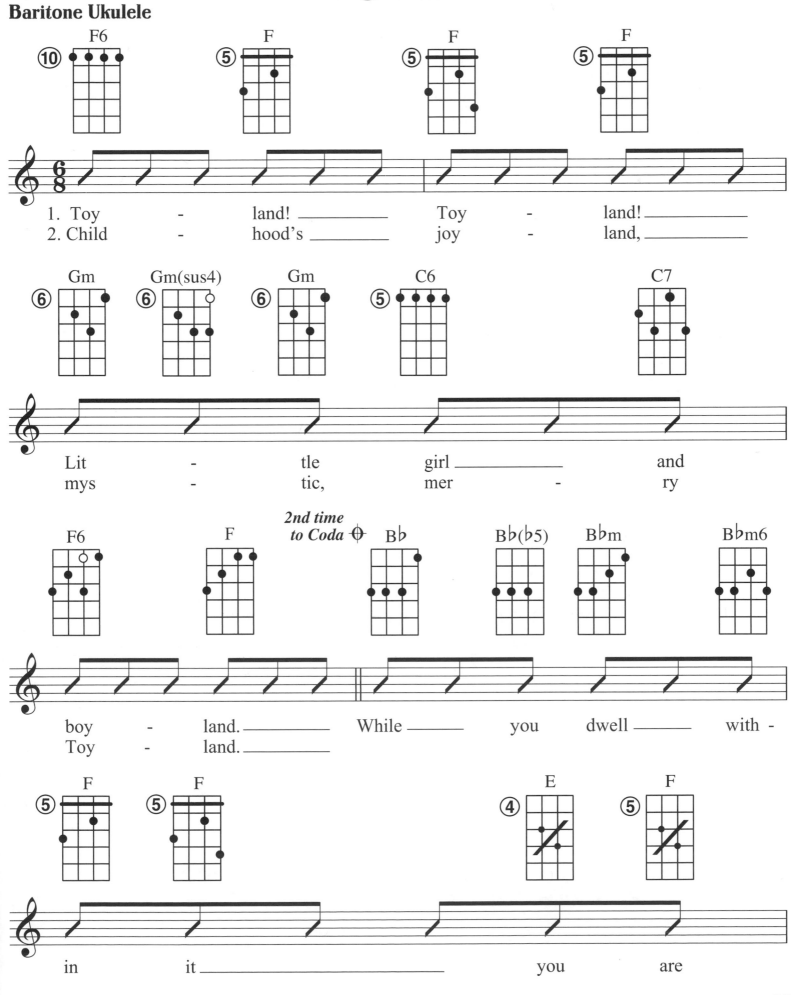

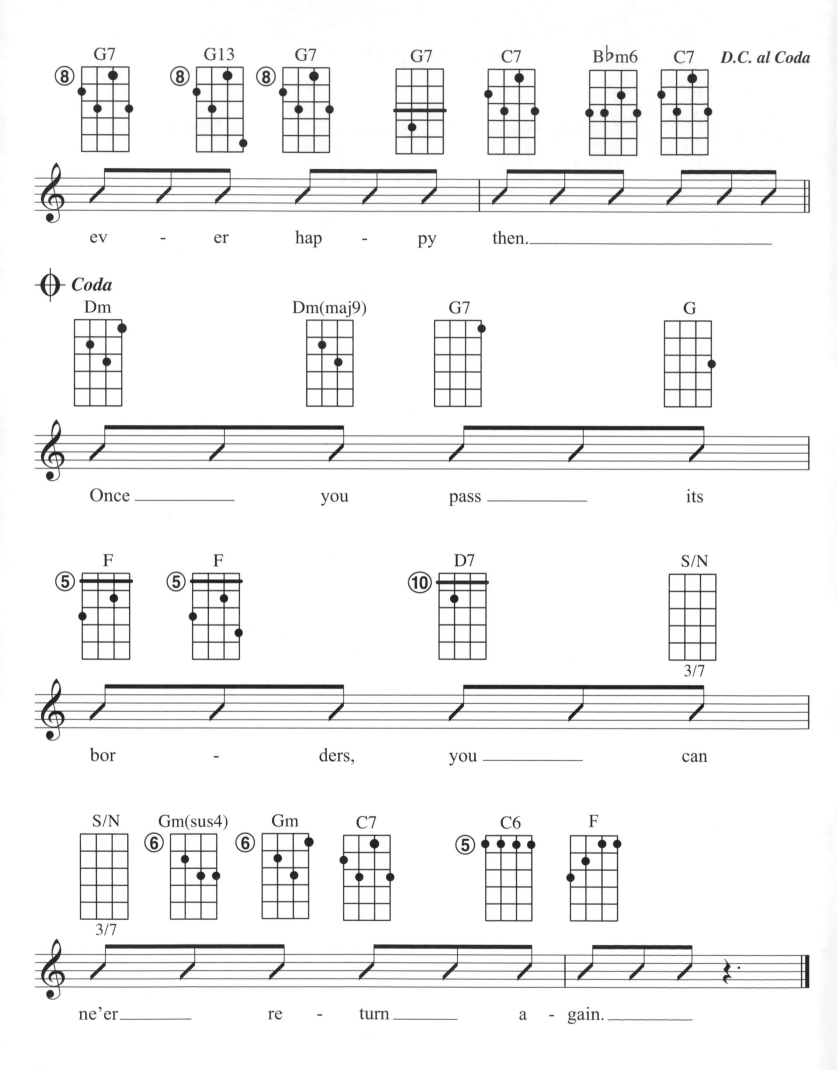

TUM BALALAIKA

Traditional

Questions and answers. Riddles and puzzles. The treasury of folk music is rich with such challenges, and "Tum Balalaika" is a fine example. This Yiddish folk song, probably of Russian origin, tells of a young man who wonders whom he should marry. He sets forth a series of riddles to a young maiden, apparently with the idea that if she answers correctly she is the one for him. Here are some of the questions he asks. Her answers are in parentheses:

What can grow without rain? (*stone*). What can burn and never end? (*love*). Cry without tears? (*heart*). Higher than a house? (*chimney*). Swifter than a mouse? (*cat*). Deeper than a well? (*Torah*), etc.

Another popular folk ballad tells of a child who outwits the devil in a lively give-and-take exchange. The questions and answers are much like those in "Tum Balalaika":

> *You must answer me questions nine*
>
> *Sing ninety-nine and ninety.*
>
> *To see if you're God's or one of mine*
>
> *Or if you are the weaver's bonnie …*

Similar songs pose questions about a cherry that has no stone, a chicken that has no bone, a rain without an end, a baby with no crying, or the Scottish ballad that asks "Who will glove my hand… shoe my foot… kiss my ruby lips when you are gone?"

No question about it, in traditional music conundrums abound.

Tum Balalaika

Baritone Ukulele

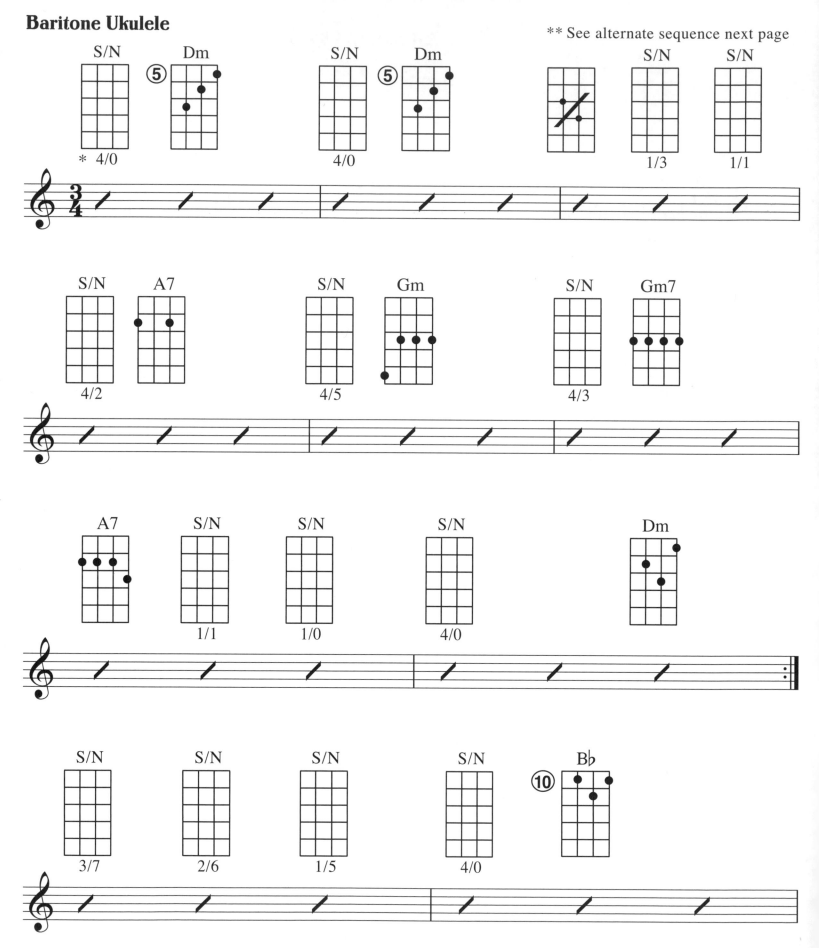

* Each S/N note on the 4th string is contained in the chord that follows it.

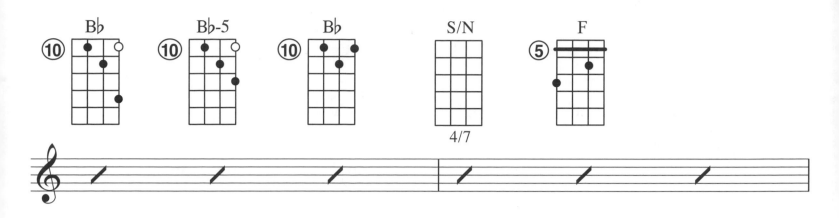

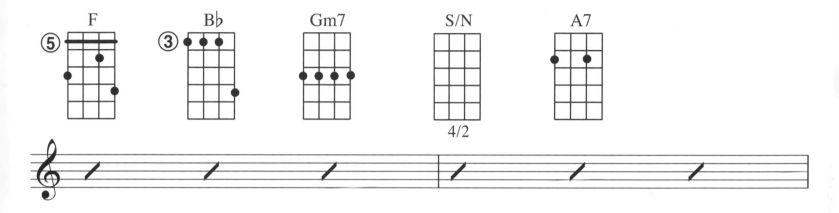

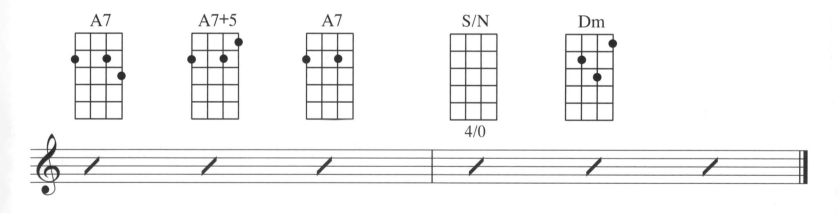

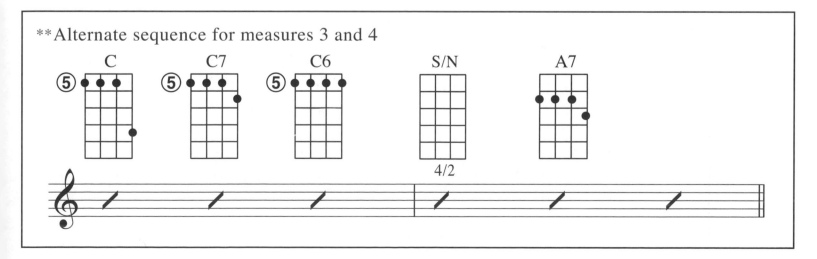

**Alternate sequence for measures 3 and 4

TWELVE-BAR BLUES

Traditional

The title of this arrangement doesn't refer to a pub crawl of a dozen saloons, but rather to the traditional blues format of 12 measures. Considered to be a uniquely American invention, the blues sprang from the rural south and gained popularity with the early recordings of the 1900s. Since then, the form has spawned hundreds if not thousands of songs, as well as songs with "Blues" in the title that may not adhere to the strict "true blue" 12-bar pattern.

Although there are innumerable variations, blues songs typically follow the chord progression found in this arrangement. Lyrics for this sequence often repeat the first line followed by a different third line. For example:

Awful lonesome, all alone and blue,

awful lonesome, all alone and blue;

ain't got nobody to tell my troubles to.

The influence of blues can be felt in American music from folk, to jazz, to rock 'n' roll, and far beyond. The style is distinctive, yet varied. It can be the haunting strums of a guitar, the bent notes of a harmonica, or the plaintive wail of a Dixieland trumpet. The lyrics encompass not just the sad and the bad, the tough times and miseries, but even brighter emotions too.

One of my favorite pictures clipped from a newspaper shows a seated aging black gentleman with his arm resting on the top of an electric guitar and a harmonica clamped in a holder around his neck. The caption reads, "If it ain't been in a pawn shop, it can't play the blues."

But no need to run out and hock your ukulele. You'll do just fine with the following arrangement. And if a few dark clouds happen to come your way—and let's hope that's not often—tune up, settle down, and purge the feeling by writing your own blues.

Playing note: Many of the E chords contain the melody on the 2nd string. The single notes and final E9 chord in the last measure can be played while holding the E chord.

Twelve-Bar Blues

Baritone Ukulele

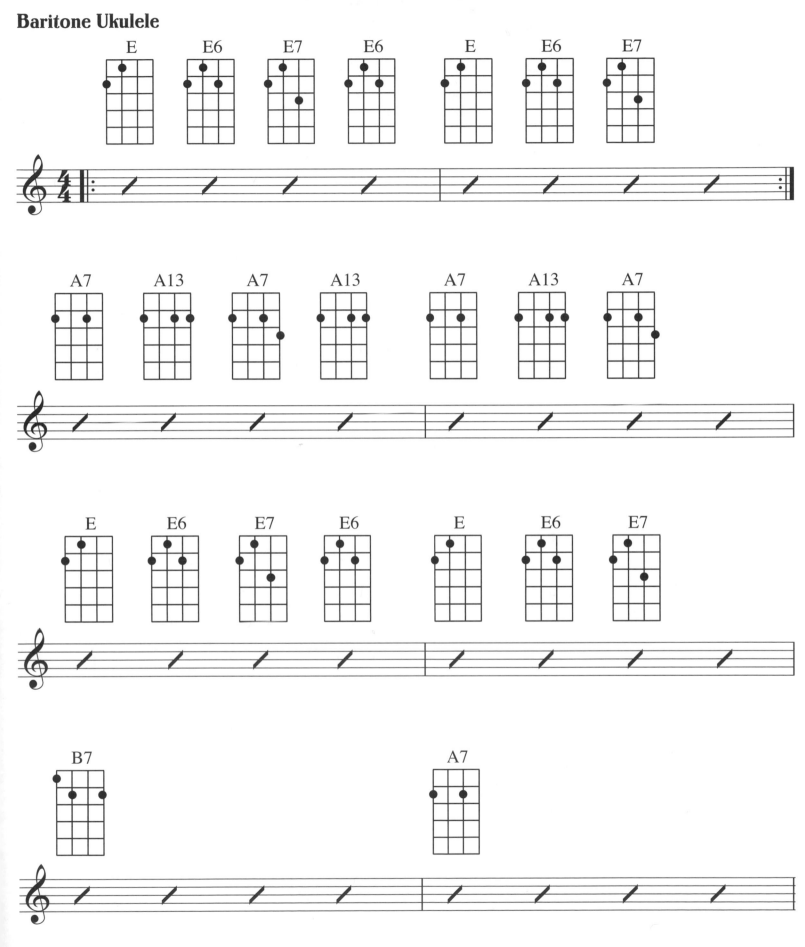

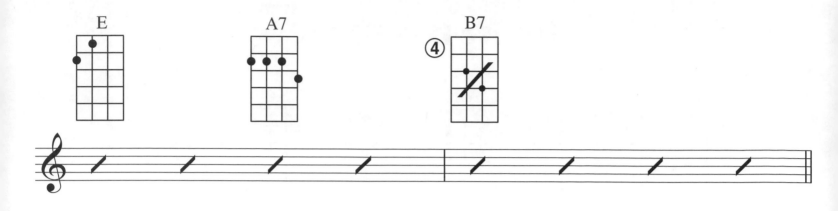

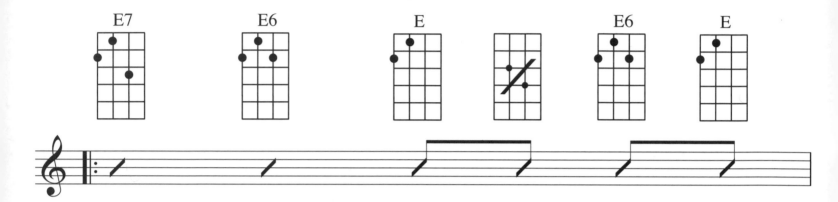

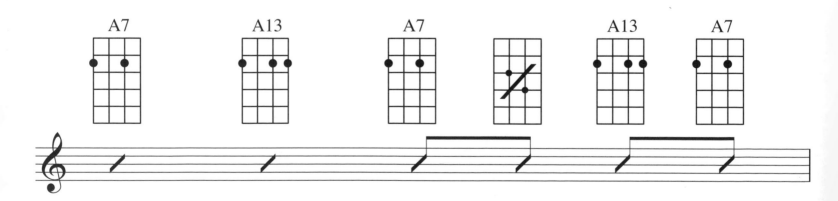

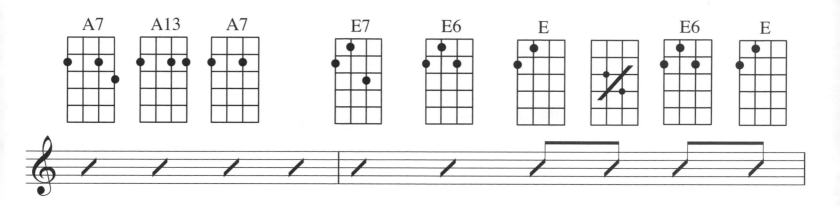

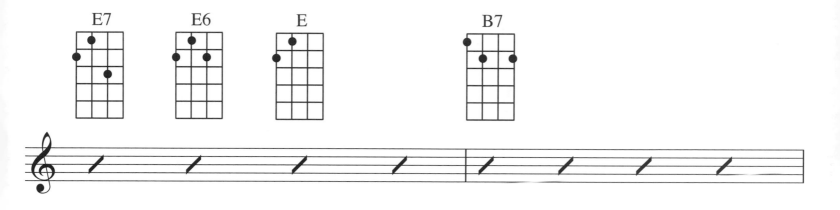

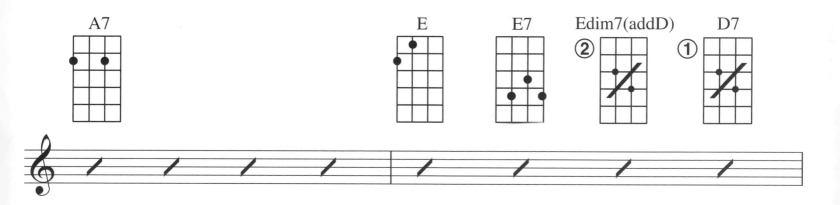

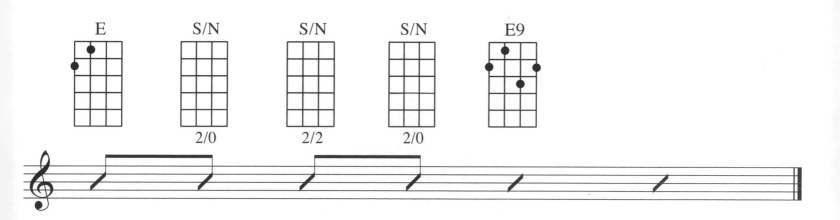

WANG WANG BLUES

(1921)

Words by LEO WOOD
Music by HENRY BUSSE,
"BUSTER" JOHNSON, and GUS MUELLER

Songs with "blues" in the title have poured forth in what seems to be an unceasing succession. Their popularity continues right up to the present day, and every imaginable misfortune and tale of woe has been set to words and music.

Despite the lamenting lyrics of this song, there's a certain playfulness about them that belies genuine melancholy. Nor is the song a true blues in the sense of following a 12-bar format. Moreover, there's an implied bounce to the music that overrides any sense of a woeful dirge.

Leo Wood, who also wrote the lyrics to "Somebody Stole My Gal," has been introduced elsewhere in this collection with the arrangement of that song. Other than Henry Busse, German born and a trumpeter in Paul Whiteman's orchestra, not much is known about Wood's other music collaborators.

There may be some significance to the "Wang Wang" in the title, but if there is, it's elusive. What is known is that the song's sheet music was a mega-seller in 1921!

Wang Wang Blues

Baritone Ukulele

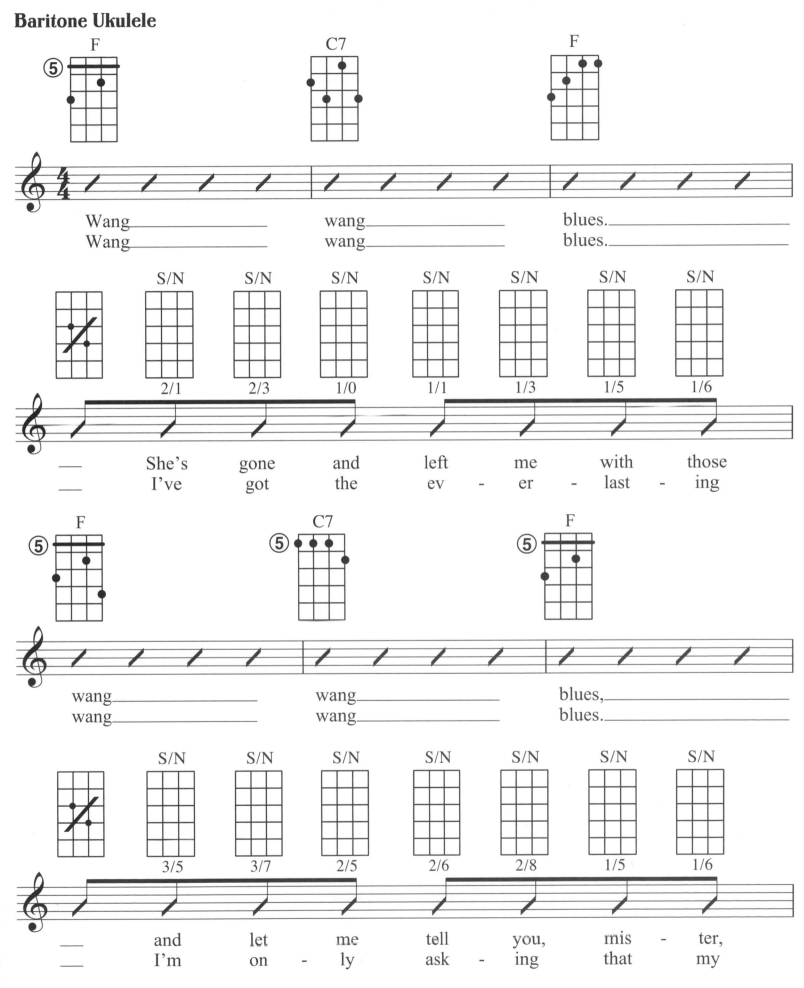

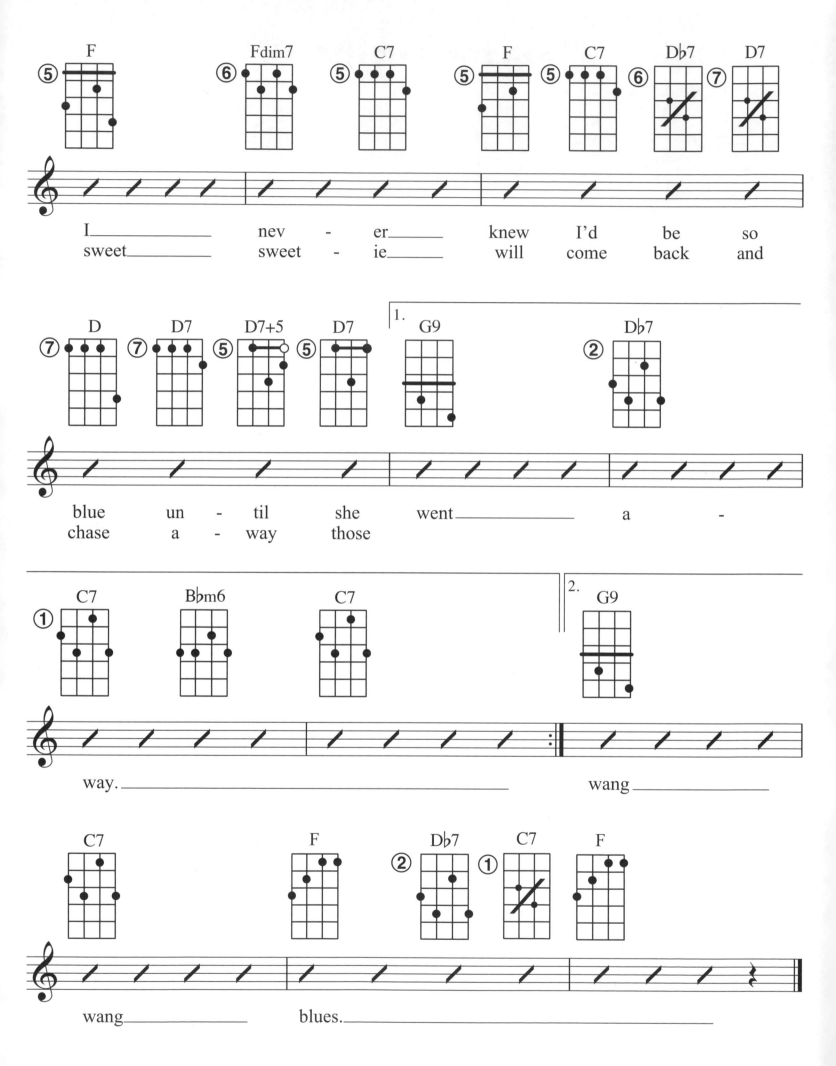

THE WORLD IS WAITING FOR THE SUNRISE

(1919)

Words by EUGENE LOCKHART
Music by ERNEST SEITZ

Songs of hopeful optimism sprang up immediately following the close of World War I. Patriotic songs were temporarily shelved, war clouds were parted, rays of sunshine broke though, and anticipation of a bright new future emerged. Here our lyricist rose to the occasion. He is better known as Hollywood actor Gene Lockhart, who appeared in such films as the 1938 version of *The Christmas Carol* and the Oscar-winning blockbuster of 1944, *Going My Way*. He also was featured in another award-winning movie, the 1947 Christmas favorite *Miracle On 34th Street*. In this film, Lockhart portrays the beleaguered judge in the Santa Claus trial scenes. He also appeared as the celestrial bookkeeper in the 1956 film version of *Carousel*.

Seitz, a classical concert pianist and a Canadian, as was Lockhart, supposedly composed the tune when he was only 12. Embarrassed to be associated with popular music, Seitz used a pseudonym when the song was first published. Of the song's many recorded versions perhaps the best known is the million-seller by guitarist Les Paul and vocalist Mary Ford relcased in 1949.

The World Is Waiting for the Sunrise

Baritone Ukulele

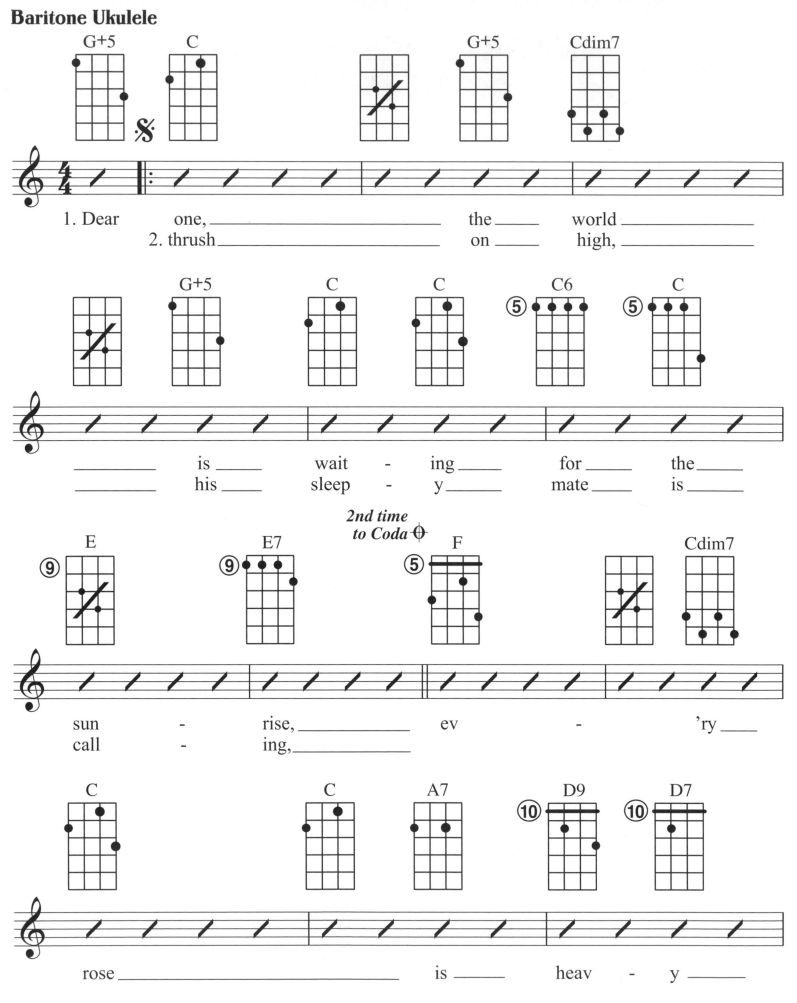

1. Dear _____ one, _____ the _____ world _____
2. thrush _____ on _____ high, _____

_____ is _____ wait - ing _____ for _____ the _____
_____ his _____ sleep - y _____ mate _____ is _____

sun - rise, _____ ev - 'ry _____
call - ing, _____

rose _____ is _____ heav - y _____

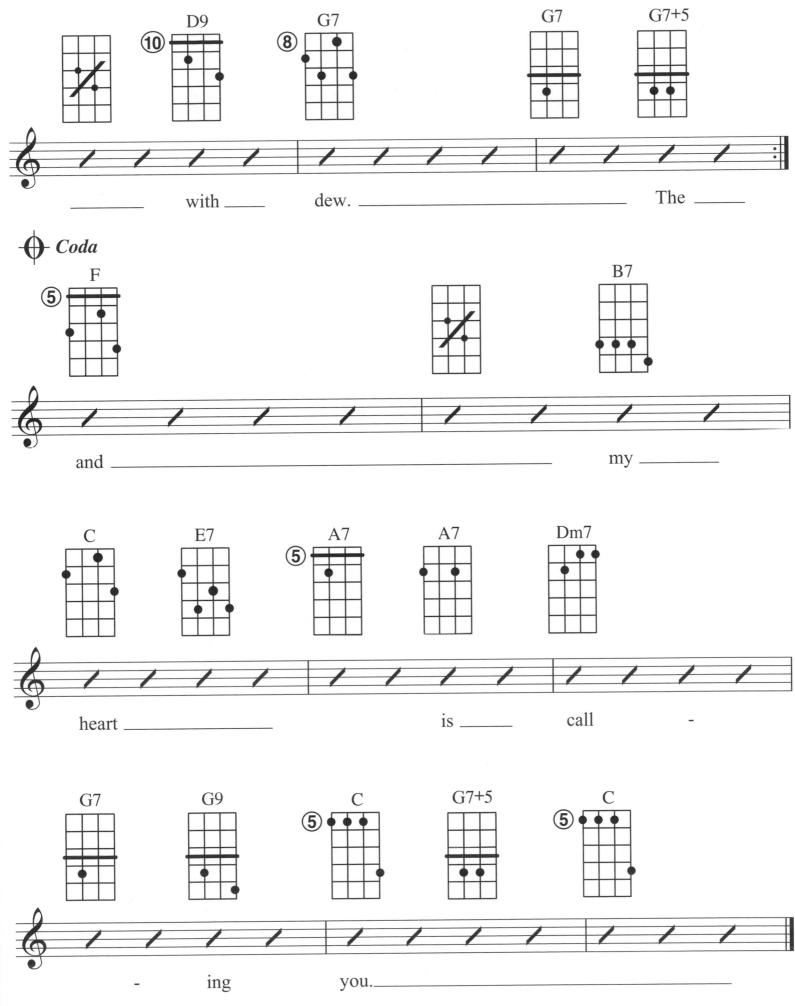

YOU TELL ME YOUR DREAMS

(1908)

Words by SEYMOUR RICE AND ALBERT H. BROWN

Music by CHARLES N. DANIELS

Only the chorus of this song is included with the solos in this collection. The words are romantic, perhaps a little teasing, and the music gently captures that feeling. But what of the verses, and there are several. Time was when verses were common. Today, few survive. Exceptions occur, and in rare instances those verses are more appealing than the choruses themselves. Such, however, is not the case here. Like "Dear Old Girl," there's a melancholy undertone that comes with the advance of the lyrics. The verses tell of a young boy and girl who exchange their affection by revealing tender dreams they have for each other. As time moves on that love is realized in marriage. But then comes the Victorian preoccupation with tragedy, and the little girl, now a woman and wife, passes from life's scene. For obvious reasons, these sad verses are typically omitted by most performers, and unlike the lovely words and melody of the chorus, they are forgotten and have vanished into obscurity.

Daniels wrote under a variety of pseudonyms, one of which was Neil Morét. His compositions include "On Moonlight Bay," "Sweet and Lovely," "Chlo-e," and "Moonlight and Roses."

You Tell Me Your Dream

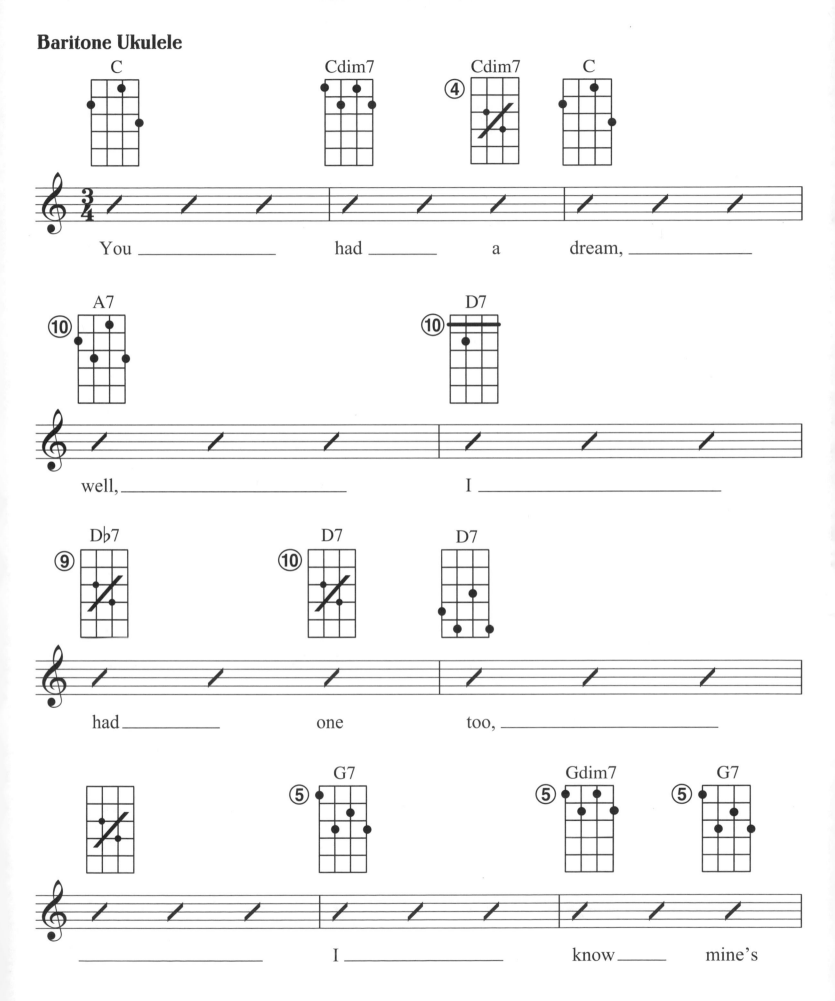

Baritone Ukulele

101

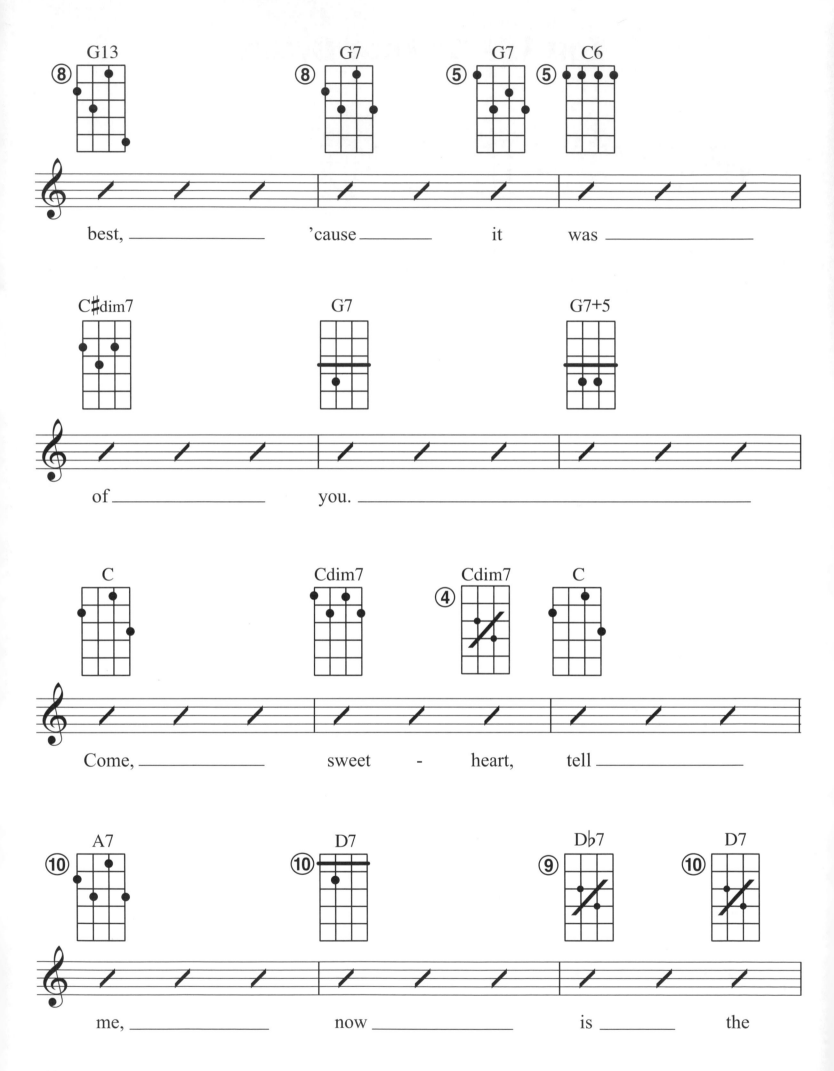

best, _____ 'cause _____ it was _____

of _____ you. _____

Come, _____ sweet - heart, tell _____

me, _____ now _____ is _____ the

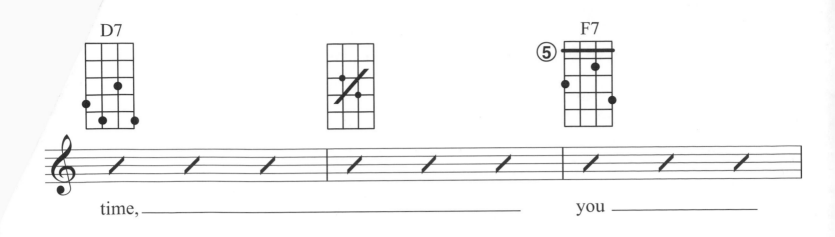

time, _____ you _____

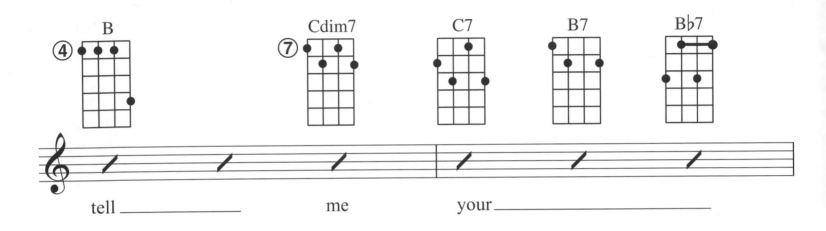

tell _____ me your _____

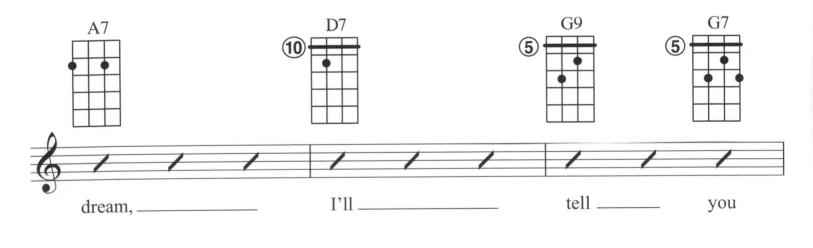

dream, _____ I'll _____ tell _____ you

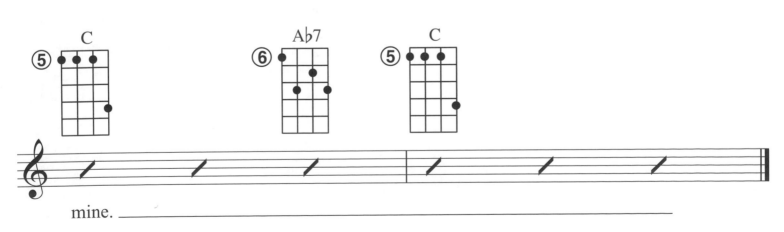

mine. _____

More Great Books from Dick Sheridan...

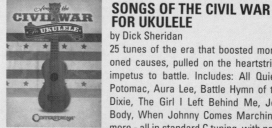